The Quest for Faithfulness

The Quest for Faithfulness

A Memoir

HELMUT HARTMANN

Translated and Edited by Kurt K. Hendel
Foreword by David Ansley Mote

RESOURCE *Publications* · Eugene, Oregon

THE QUEST FOR FAITHFULNESS
A Memoir

Copyright © 2019 Kurt K. Hendel. All rights reserved. Except for brief quotations in critical publications or reviews, no part of this book may be reproduced in any manner without prior written permission from the publisher. Write: Permissions, Wipf and Stock Publishers, 199 W. 8th Ave., Suite 3, Eugene, OR 97401.

Resource Publications
An Imprint of Wipf and Stock Publishers
199 W. 8th Ave., Suite 3
Eugene, OR 97401

www.wipfandstock.com

PAPERBACK ISBN: 978-1-5326-5808-2
HARDCOVER ISBN: 978-1-5326-5809-9
EBOOK ISBN: 978-1-5326-5810-5

Manufactured in the U.S.A.   MARCH 20, 2019

Scripture quotations are from the New Revised Standard Version Bible, copyright © 1989 National Council of the Churches of Christ in the United States of America. Used by permission. All rights reserved worldwide.

When scriptural passages are quoted from the NRSV this is noted in the text. When there is no such notation, the translation is of the scriptural text as it is quoted in the original manuscript.

"Als ich in weissem Krankenzimmer der Charité," in: Bertolt Brecht, Werke. Grosse kommentierte Berliner und Frankfurter Ausgabe, Band 15: Gedichte 5. © Bertolt-Brecht-Erben / Suhrkamp Verlag 1993. All rights with and controlled through Suhrkamp Verlag Berlin.

Excerpt from: Bertolt Brecht, Der gute Mensch von Sezuan, in: ibid., Werke. Grosse kommentierte Berliner und Frankfurter Ausgabe, Band 6: Stücke 6. © Bertolt-Brecht-Erben / Suhrkamp Verlag 1989. All rights with and controlled through Suhrkamp Verlag Berlin.

Sincere thanks to Christiane for forty-three years together

Contents

Foreword by David Ansley Mote | xi
Acknowledgments | xv

1932 A Man with a Sign | 1
1933 The Parsonage in Burgörner | 4
1934 Two Chopped-off Noses | 7
1935 The Teacher's Residence, Berlin | 9
1936 Nappian and Neucke | 13
1937 My Esteemed Uncle Karl | 15
1938 A Jewish Store Destroyed | 17
1939 Vacation in Trockenborn | 19
1940 Birthdays, Hamsters, and May Beetles | 21
1941 Expatriates in Our Village | 23
1942 We Visit Our Great-grandfather | 25
1943 Berlin Evacuation | 28
1944 For the Sake of Victory | 31
1945 Liberation | 33
1946 The 400th Anniversary of Martin Luther's Death | 36
1947 I Want to Be a Farmer | 41
1948 At the Stephaneum | 43
1949 Two German States | 46

Contents

1950 A Night Hike | 49
1951 Campus Ministry in Halle | 51
1952 My Conversions | 54
1953 June 17, 1953 in Halle | 57
1954 Hamburg, Gateway to the World | 62
1955 Vicar in Lindau | 64
1956 Seminary in Brandenburg | 66
1957 The Black Pump | 69
1958 First Pastorate, Mücheln | 74
1959 Bliss with Tent and Bicycle | 77
1960 Summer along the Volga | 79
1961 The Berlin Wall | 82
1962 A Stormy February Night | 84
1963 A Star Falls from Heaven's Vault | 86
1964 Construction Soldiers | 88
1965 Demanding a New Eastern Policy | 90
1966 Who Are You? | 93
1967 Pastor in Lutherstadt Eisleben | 95
1968 End of the Prague Spring | 98
1969 Drama after Klaus's Birth | 100
1970 Adventures in Church Renovation | 102
1971 Ecclesiastical Tourism | 105
1972 A Christian in Socialism | 107
1973 An Inter-congregational Reform Circle | 109
1974 Local Ecumenism | 111
1975 The Peasants' War | 113
1976 The Beacon from Zeitz | 116
1977 A Congregation of Actors | 119
1978 To Halle as Superintendent | 121

Contents

1979   Halle is Better than Its Reputation | 123
1980   A Delegation to Canada | 126
1981   On the Way Together | 129
1982   Swords into Plowshares | 132
1983   Citizen Rights Groups in the Church | 135
1984   Unexpected Consequences | 137
1985   The Service of Visitation | 139
1986   City Mission Pastor, Erfurt | 142
1987   A City that Deals Justly | 144
1988   Remain and Resist | 146
1989   The Miracle | 148
1990   A Hope Learns to Walk | 151
1991   Day of Unity | 154
1992   In Polish East Prussia | 156
1993   Melting Heart | 158
1994   To Jesus's Table | 161
1995   A Christmas Story | 163
1996   The Compassionate Romanian | 167
1997   Crooked Tree—Erect Walk | 169
1998   The Three Informers of King Herod | 172
1999   An Encounter on Children's Day | 174
2000   A Fifty-year Reunion | 176
2001   Suddenly Gone | 178
2002   A Good Conclusion | 181

Bibliography | 185

Foreword

I MET HELMUT HARTMANN at the Baptist Church in Moscow in the summer of 1960. I was with a group of a dozen young Americans in the Soviet Union as part of an exchange program arranged by our State Department and the Soviet Foreign Ministry. During that Sunday service an announcement was made in English welcoming foreign visitors and informing us of an opportunity to learn about the church in a meeting after the service. Our whole group attended along with dozens of others who had attended the service.

A pastor of the church who had studied in England spoke to us. Judging from how people were dressed in those days (when it was easy to spot whether people were from east or west of the Iron Curtain), all but one of the visitors in the room were from the West. Sitting next to me was a young man from somewhere behind the Iron Curtain. I would have assumed he was from the USSR except for the fact that the meeting was for foreign visitors to the church.

As soon as the meeting concluded I introduced myself and asked where he was from. I was surprised to hear that he was a Lutheran pastor from East Germany. Helmut and I spent the rest of that day together, and we began a correspondence that went on for forty years. After the first year it mostly consisted of annual letters. Every year during Advent Helmut wrote a thoughtful two-page letter that went to family and friends from all over, and he always added a hand-written personal note to me.

In 1975 I visited the Hartmanns in Eisleben. When I learned he would be part of a delegation from the Evangelical Church in East Germany to the United Church of Canada in 1980, I flew to Toronto and spent a day with him. We discussed whether it would make trouble for him if I were to visit him in Halle, and he assured me that it should be possible to get government permission to do so. That visit in the summer of 1980 turned out to be a wonderful week staying in the Hartmanns' home.

Foreword

In 2002 I sent my annual letter and did not receive one in return. When the 2003 letter did not come I wondered whether his Parkinsons was the reason (see Chapter 1997, "Crooked Tree—Erect Walk") or whether something else had happened. I continued to write each year, and my letters did not come back as undeliverable.

In 2013 I experienced a very strong sense that if Helmut were still alive I needed to see him again. I remembered that his daughter Sabine had wanted to be a pediatrician. I entered her name and Kinderärztin (pediatrician) in an online search, and her name came up with no email address but with the address of her medical practice. I mailed a letter to her. Sabine remembered me and wrote back catching me up on her parents' situation. Her father had been unable to write for several years.

My wife Nadia and I visited Helmut and Christiane in their home in Dessau in the summer of 2014. Parkinsons had taken quite a toll on him physically but he was still very sharp mentally. We were all grateful to be together once again. Helmut gave me a copy of *Unsere 70 Jahre* (*Our Seventy Years*, the original title of his memoir).

With my limited ability in German it took me many months to read it. It was clear to me that it should be available to a wider audience. I wrote to Sabine that I would like to see if I could find a way to get it published. At the end of November 2015, Helmut signed a hand-written note granting me permission to pursue publication in the USA. He died February 20, 2016.

Helmut wrote the memoir for his children and grandchildren. He had no need to include things they all knew very well. A question some readers might wonder about is how he and Christiane met. In 1958 Helmut's sister married Christiane's brother, with Helmut's father presiding as pastor. Helmut and Christiane met at that wedding. Just a year later Helmut's father presided at their wedding.

Some may also be puzzled to read in the chapter "1945 Liberation" that the American occupying force left the area where the Hartmanns lived and were replaced by the Soviet army. This came about because the victorious Western powers, France, Great Britain, and the United States, decided that Berlin should not be occupied only by the Soviets. In exchange for having a share in the occupation of Berlin, which had been liberated by the Soviets, the three Western powers turned over to the USSR part of the territory they had liberated.

Helmut Hartmann's memoir is not only a personal, family story. Rather, Helmut consistently comments on the contexts, events, and personalities

Foreword

that impacted his life. The memoir is, therefore, a persistent engagement of Helmut's personal story with the historical events in the context in which he lived. That context was one of the most dramatic and challenging periods in German history and particularly in the history of individual Christians and of the Christian church in Germany. It was the time of the Nazi regime and of the German Democratic Republic. During both of those periods, all residents in the German territories and surely all Christians had to make crucial decisions about their identity, their values, and their way of life. Helmut Hartmann's memoir is the story of one man's quest to be faithful to his faith convictions and his sense of humanity when those convictions and that sense were challenged in radical ways.

I am deeply grateful to Professor Hendel for taking on the task of translation and for adding the many explanatory footnotes. Reading the memoir in English I realize what a big task it was and how much I missed when I read the original.

DAVID ANSLEY MOTE

Acknowledgments

I WISH TO EXPRESS my appreciation and thanks to Pastor Helmut Hartmann for his willingness to share his memoir with a wider public and to his family who have supported that willingness; to Pastor David Mote, who was in possession of a copy of the memoir and invited me to evaluate its potential for publication; to Wipf and Stock Publishers for their interest in the memoir, particularly to Matthew Wimer, Assistant Managing Editor, Daniel Lanning, Editorial Administrative Assistant, and George Callihan, typesetter, for their gracious assistance during the production of the translation; and to Ms. Nadia Ilyin for her expert copy editing.

KURT K. HENDEL

1932

A Man with a Sign

A MAN IS STANDING on the Potsdamer Platz in Berlin on a cold February day in the year 1932 with a sign on his belly: "I am looking for any kind of work." He has pulled his hat deeply down on his face, as if he were ashamed. The newspaper sellers around him shout, "The six-million mark has been passed in Germany for the first time. 6,127,000 people are unemployed!" Advertisements on pillars call attention to Gerhard Hauptmann's[1] drama, *Before Sunset*. The premiere is to occur at the German Theater on the occasion of Hauptmann's seventieth birthday. Bertolt Brecht's[2] *The Mother*, a dramatization of the novel by Maxim Gorky,[3] is being presented at the Berlin Comedy House. Hans Fallada's[4] novel, *Little Man—What Now?* is being promoted in bookstores.

---

1. Gerhard Hauptmann (1862–1946) was a German writer who produced both dramas and comedies. He was awarded the Nobel Prize in Literature in 1912 and was considered one of Germany's most important writers, also by the international community.

2. Eugen Berthold Friedrich Brecht (1898–1956), who used the name Bertolt Brecht professionally, was one of the most important and influential German playwrights and poets of the twentieth century. His literary works opposed fascism and promoted socialism.

3. Alexei Marimovich Peshkov (1868–1936), known primarily as Maxim Gorky, was a Russian writer and political activist. His writings were significantly impacted by his extensive travels throughout Russia and inspired five nominations for the Nobel Prize in Literature. As a Bolshevik Marxist, he opposed the czar, but he then also criticized the political ambitions of Vladimir Lenin (1870–1924). As a result, he was exiled from Russia but returned in 1932 at the invitation of Joseph Stalin (1878–1953).

4. Rudolf Wilhelm Friedrich Dietzen (1893–1947) published his literary works under

The Quest for Faithfulness

A little girl named Christiane is born in a hospital in Berlin-Karlshorst on this cold February 7. Her parents, Alfred and Elisabeth Kühn, order the names of their children according to the "golden alphabet."[5] Father Alfred is the first (A), then the firstborn Berthold (B); then follow Christiane (C) and Dankwart (D); and after mother Elisabeth (E) follow Friederike (F) and Gebhard (G).

When Christiane is born, her father, a secondary school teacher, is writing his book, *Matter in Atoms and Stars*.[6] In amazement he speaks of the "smallest and greatest objects in which matter occurs . . ." and admires the mental labor of researchers before our time. "The pleasure that fills a lover of the arts when he listens to a symphony by Beethoven or views a master portrait of Rembrandt can also fill the person who considers the work of scientists."

Twenty-four hours earlier, a son has been born to Wilhelm and Ruth Hartmann in the parsonage in Burgörner, in the territory of Mansfeld. He is their second child. Like his siblings, he receives a Germanic name, Helmut. His sisters are named Gudrun and Irmgard and his younger brother Günter. Their father considers himself to be a "religious socialist" with regard to the political and social challenges in his industrial-class congregation, in which he experiences the devastating consequences of extensive unemployment in near proximity. A few days after the birth of his son Helmut, he writes in the foreword of his book about *Heinrich Zschokke's Hours of Devotion*:[7] "The nations experience distress and perplexity once again. Human beings are anxious for comfort and help. The holy God, who speaks a powerful word in the midst of the shocking realities of the present world, rules over them!"

Who hears God speaking in shocking social and political realities? An election campaign for the new president of the German Reich rages on.

---

the pseudonym Hans Fallada. He struggled with the effects of a severe accident and serious illness and became addicted to medications. In spite of these challenges, Fallada was able to work as a journalist and become a productive writer, especially after 1928 when his drug addiction was controlled. He also married, and the marriage brought greater stability into his life. *Little Man—What Now?* was a literary success and was made into a movie in the United States.

5. The original reads "Güldne ABC." Martin Luther called Psalm 119 "das güldene ABC" because the sections of the psalm are labeled according to the Hebrew alphabet. The "golden alphabet" thus means "in alphabetical order."

6. Kühn, *Die Materie*.

7. Hartmann, *Zschokkes Stunden der Andacht*.

A Man with a Sign

Hindenburg,[8] Hitler,[9] Duesterberg,[10] and Thälmann[11] are considered to be the leading candidates. The aged Hindenburg prevails one more time. But for how long? What can he still achieve at age eighty-five? Hitler's followers are on standby.[12] Will 1932 be the last year of the Weimar Republic? How prepared are Christians, Idealists, Socialists, Democrats, Communists, art lovers, academics, and teachers for the threatening upheavals of their society?

The man with the sign "I am looking for any kind of work" pulls his hat down on his face, as if he were ashamed.

---

8. Paul von Hindenburg (1847–1934) commanded the German armies during part of World War I and served as president of the Weimar Republic.

9. Adolf Hitler (1889–1945) was the leader of the National Socialist German Workers Party, generally referred to as the Nazi Party, and was chancellor of Germany from 1933 until 1945.

10. Theodor Duesterberg (1875–1950) was an officer in the German army during World War I and subsequently became a leader of the Stahlhelm, Bund der Frontsoldaten, a political party composed primarily of former soldiers. Because of its nationalistic and monarchical perspectives, the party opposed the Weimar Republic. Duesterberg was ardently anti-Semitic and persisted in his anti-Semitism even after he learned of his Jewish ancestry. He ran as a candidate for the presidency of Germany in the 1932 elections. The news of his ancestry resulted in little support, and he withdrew from the subsequent runoff election. Hartmann mistakenly refers to Duesterberg as Duisenberg.

11. Ernst Thälmann (1886–1944) was the leader of the Communist Party in Germany during the Weimar Republic. He was arrested, imprisoned, and eventually executed by the Nazis.

12. Hartmann uses the phrase "Gewehr bei Fuss."

1933

The Parsonage in Burgörner

SINCE 1905 THE EVANGELICAL[1] parsonage has been situated where the water mill of the manor of Burgörner operated for many decades. An old wall made of large, black cinder blocks, which marked the border of our garden on the east, was for us children a mysterious witness from the past. The stories of Karoline von Dacherröden,[2] which our mother told us, occurred in the adjacent castle park. Karoline had become engaged to Wilhelm von Humboldt in this park. We children still saw the remains of

---

1. The German word Evangelisch is consistently translated as "Evangelical" throughout the text. The term is not intended to denote contemporary Evangelicalism, which is an important expression of Christianity, particularly in the Americas. Evangelisch or "Evangelical," as it is used in this volume, refers to the Lutheran, Reformed, or Union Churches in Germany that consider themselves to be heirs of the sixteenth-century Reformation. The Union Churches resulted from a joining of Lutheran and Reformed communities in the so-called Prussian Union of 1817. The Evangelische Kirche in Deutschland (EKD) is a federation of twenty German territorial churches representing these traditions. Theologians, programs, and organizations related to these churches are also referred to as Evangelisch.

2. Karoline von Dacherröden (1766–1829) was a member of an old Thuringian noble family who married Wilhelm von Humboldt (1767–1835). The couple had eight children, although they lived apart periodically. She traveled throughout Europe, was an ardent patron of the arts, and carried on a lively correspondence with contemporary politicians, scholars, and writers. As Hartmann notes, she lived in Burgörner for a time during her youth.

the "love nest." Goethe,[3] Schiller,[4] Körner,[5] the world traveler Alexander von Humboldt,[6] and many other famous people strolled in this park. We grew up in such a distinguished neighborhood.

Our parents were shocked by Hitler's rise to power in 1933 and from the very beginning recognized the tragic consequences for church and society. Nevertheless, they strove to create a pleasant, safe home in the house and garden for us four children, who were born in the parsonage between 1930 and 1935. However, they did not want to isolate us. We played with children from the neighborhood, whose fathers worked in industry or on the manor. There were no social class distinctions among us. We welcomed the son of a horse-stable worker in the same manner as the children of a director of a foundry, of the lord of the manor, or of a factory worker.

As we grew older, our sphere of activity expanded. We romped through the large castle park, built huts behind thick bushes or on trees, slowly conquered the lower village and later the upper village. However, the parsonage and its garden remained our home. Our mother spent much time with us, played and sang with us, made things with us, painted with us, and took walks with us. She also prayed with us at bedtime in the evening. When doing so, she did not hide needs and danger from us children. We learned from the evening prayers that there was civil war in Spain and many people died daily. We learned that our grandfather in Kahla suffered from a terrible form of diabetes and died from it. I could not comprehend why such a terrible illness was called diabetes.[7] After all, sugar is something beautiful

3. Johann Wolfgang von Goethe (1749–1832) was one of Germany's most influential writers and poets. He also published scientific works and produced a large number of drawings. In addition to his literary work, he served as a civil servant and as managing director of the theater in Weimar.

4. Johann Christoph Friedrich von Schiller (1759–1805) was a German dramatist, poet, playwright, philosopher, and historian who, together with Goethe, made Weimar the intellectual center of Germany and fostered what is generally referred to as Weimar Classicism.

5. Carl Theodor Körner (1791–1813) was born in Dresden but lived in Vienna for a time where he met Alexander von Humboldt, Karl Wilhelm Friedrich Schlegel (1772–1829), and other literary figures. He became a writer himself and wrote dramas, operas, and poetry. He also served as a soldier in the Napoleonic Wars during which he lost his life.

6. Alexander von Humboldt (1769–1859) was a gifted intellectual and explorer who traveled extensively, particularly in the Americas. He was especially interested in studying the natural environment and noted the reality of climate change induced by human activity. His contributions to the scientific world were diverse and highly influential.

7. Zuckerkrankheit literally means "sugar illness."

for children! When Aunt Else from Hamburg visited us, there was always a special addition to the evening prayer. She went to each bed and made five different faces. We laughed heartily as a result.

I am still puzzled how our mother was able to dedicate so much time to us children in addition to caring for the large household and participating in the voluntary activities in the congregation (youth groups, women's circles, choir, and playing the organ). In the evening, when we children were all in bed, our mother sometimes played the piano and sang with her beautiful voice *Die schöne Müllerin* or the *Winterreise* by Franz Schubert;[8] the *Uhr* or *Herr Heinrich sass am Finkenheerd* by Carl Löwe;[9] or love songs by Hermann Löns.[10] Our mother could laugh in a wonderful way. She often laughed to the point of tears. It was only after I became older that I recognized that our mother already knew about all the atrocities since January 1933: namely, that Nazis attacked Jews, Communists, Social Democrats, Liberal Democrats, and Christians, also nearby in the territory of Mansfeld. And yet she could be so cheerful with us. It must, no doubt, have been connected to her faith: "In you is joy in all suffering..."[11]

---

8. Franz Schubert (1797-1828) was a talented Austrian composer whose diverse body of work includes songs, symphonies, operas, piano and chamber music, and sacred works. He is widely recognized as one of the most important nineteenth-century composers. *Die schöne Müllerin* and the *Winterreise* were two song cycles by Schubert.

9. Johann Gottfried Carl Löwe (1796-1869) wrote over four hundred lieder (songs) with piano accompaniment during his career as a composer, performing tenor, and conductor. While his fame has waned, his songs were quite popular during the nineteenth century. He also wrote cantatas, choral ballads, and oratorios and was a well-known touring tenor during his career.

10. Hermann Löns (1866-1914) is known particularly for his novels and poems that explore the life and landscape of the Lüneburg Heath. However, he also composed folksongs and was a natural historian and naturalist. His literary works remained popular during the twentieth century.

11. Hartmann is quoting the first two lines of a chorale text from Johann Sebastian Bach's (1685-1750) Cantata BWV 615. The first printed version of the text is in a collection of twenty Christmas carols titled *Amorum filii Dei decades duae . . . Zwantzig Weyhenachten Gesenglein* . . . The collection was published by Johannes Lindemann (c. 1550-c.1633) in Erfurt in 1594.

1934

Two Chopped-off Noses

UNTIL THE BEGINNING OF the war we experienced solemn funeral services in the village. After the funeral service in the home of the deceased, there was a funeral procession through the whole village, past the church, and up to the cemetery on the Hollerberg behind the ruin of the castle. We children of the pastor could observe the funeral procession from the window. The brass band led the procession and played somber melodies. The brass musicians all wore the brown uniforms of Nazi storm troops. All organizations had been incorporated into the Nazi system by 1934.

Our father walked behind the brass band in his black gown and with a beret on his head. The hearse with two stately horses that belonged to the farmer Goldschmidt followed him. The horses and hearse were covered with black cloths. The casket, decorated with many flowers and wreaths, was on the hearse. Miners, in their dress uniforms, walked next to the wagon, three on the left side and three on the right side. The closest relatives walked right behind the wagon, and the village community followed them. We remained at the window until the brass band returned. They then played joyful melodies and went to the Wagner or the Bartel Restaurant. After so much blowing, the thirst had to be stilled!

The police officer Remus "ruled" in the village at that time. He had accommodated politically in order to remain in office. However, he also wanted to maintain his good relationship with the pastorate. One day he received a disconcerting command. He was supposed to confiscate the red index cards of the Confessing Church that were in the parsonage. The names of the members of the congregation, who did not want to accept the leadership claims of the Nazis in the church, were recorded on those cards. The police officer was now supposed to confiscate these index cards. However, our parents had already been warned beforehand about this. As the dignified, tall, and burly servant of the state headed for the parsonage, the index cards had already been wrapped in our mother's apron for some time. Our mother waited for the moment when the police officer entered the main entrance of the parsonage. She then rushed quickly through the yard door across the street to the neighbors and requested that the index cards be safely hidden. The neighbors helped, of course, even though the husband had to wear the brown uniform as the leader of the brass band. Our mother returned quickly to the parsonage, entered the office of our father "innocently," and clarified for the police officer that the index cards were no longer in the parsonage. The police officer indicated that he was satisfied with this assurance and left the parsonage relieved.

A year earlier a command to search the parsonage happened in a similar harmless manner. Unknown perpetrators had knocked off the noses of Hitler and Hindenburg on the "Monument of the Revolt" on Humboldt Street. No hot trail could be discovered in spite of an immediately initiated hunt that included the search of houses, also the parsonage. The monument was removed. The stone slabs with the damaged heads of Hitler and Hindenburg were stored in the firehouse next to the parsonage until 1945. A fireman showed me these stones shortly before the end of the war. The stones disappeared a few weeks later. A resident of the village supposedly incorporated them into the pavement in front of his door with the faces pointed downward. They may still lie there even today.

1935

The Teacher's Residence, Berlin

THE KÜHN FAMILY, WITH their five children, must surely have attracted attention in the Taut housing development in Zehlendorf.[1] It must have been lively in their modern house, built at the end of the 1920s, and its small garden. The Beitl family, with three children at that time, lived across the street from them. The two mothers were sisters. Father Kühn worked as secondary school teacher of the natural sciences in the Queen Louise School, which Christiane also attended as a secondary school pupil. The children often had to change schools because of events related to the war. Father Beitl was a scholar of folklore at the university. Christiane still remembers very precisely her time in kindergarten together with Thea Beitl at the Evangelical Ernst Moritz Arndt congregation. The older the children became, the more their experiential world expanded in the sandy region between the pine forests and large lakes, such as Krumme Lanke, Schlachtensee, and Wannsee. They conquered the various parts of the metropolis of Berlin from the subway station "Uncle Tom's Cabin." Grandfather Kühn proudly guided his grandchildren through old, historical Berlin, with its castles, palaces, museums, and churches. The parents made it possible for their children to enjoy a beautiful childhood into which, however, the terrors of the war intruded periodically. In the children's memories, cheerful pictures are mixed with sad ones:

---

1. Zehlendorf is located in the southwestern part of Berlin and is one of the more affluent sections of the city.

The Quest for Faithfulness

- Of the milk boys[2] on the milk wagons drawn by horses.
- Of the baker boys who rode their bikes through the streets and filled the bread bags on the door handles.
- Of the commercial streets near the train station "Uncle Tom's Cabin," where one could admire mountains of dates and buy white radishes.

At the same time, the other pictures:

- Of bombed-out families in front of their destroyed villas in Dahlem.[3]
- Of burning cows on the meadows of the domain Dahlem that were enflamed by phosphorus bombs.
- Of wounded young soldiers who were led past without legs or arms or with serious facial wounds.

The parents knew even much more about the terrible occurrences. A statement by Max Liebermann,[4] which he supposedly made on January 30, 1933, must also have reached them: "Of course, I cannot eat as much as I want to throw up." Who knows what the Kühns and Beitls discussed in the evening when the children slept. Pastor Martin Niemöller[5] was already arrested in 1937 in nearby Dahlem. He was kept in solitary confinement in various concentration camps as a "personal prisoner of Hitler" until the end of the war. The writer Ernst Wiechert,[6] whose books were also part

---

2. The Bollejungen were boys who worked on the milk wagons that delivered milk in Berlin.

3. Dahlem was part of the Berlin borough of Zehlendorf. It remains an affluent part of the city. The Free University of Berlin is located in Dahlem.

4. Max Liebermann (1847–1935) was a German-Jewish impressionist artist whose art focused particularly on the life and work of the poor. He also produced many portraits. He apparently made this statement when the Nazis celebrated their election victory with a march through the Berlin Brandenburg Gate.

5. Friedrich Gustav Emil Martin Niemöller (1892–1984) was a Lutheran pastor and theologian who was the founder of the Pastors' Emergency League and a leading figure in the Confessing Church, which opposed the Nazi efforts to gain the support of Christians by means of the German Christian movement. Although he was imprisoned in concentration camps, he survived the Nazi period and became a proponent of recognizing and confessing the collective guilt of the German people and of pacifism after the war.

6. Ernst Wiechert (1887–1950) was a prolific writer and poet as well as a university professor. He was an opponent of the Nazi regime who protested the imprisonment of Martin Niemöller and was himself sent to the Buchenwald concentration camp, as Hartmann indicates. His imprisonment lasted four months, and he lived to criticize German society in the years immediately following the war. His novels were very popular in

of Kühn's library, was imprisoned in the Buchenwald concentration camp because he had told Göring[7] that he would no longer support the Winter Relief Fund[8] monetarily since he now had to support the Niemöller family with its many children.

It is likely that the arrest of Provost Lichtenberg[9] of the Roman Catholic St. Hedwig Cathedral and his death during his imprisonment were also discussed on the Fuchspass.[10] Provost Lichtenberg had prayed regularly and publicly for the Jews after the Kristallnacht[11] of 1938. Around that time a Jewish family with children disappeared without much attention. The family had lived as pleasant and genial neighbors on the Fuchspass. I can also imagine that an announcement in the newspaper during Advent 1942 aroused people's feelings. The poet Jochen Klepper,[12] together with his wife and daughter, committed suicide in neighboring Niklassee. His Jewish wife and Jewish daughter were supposed to report for transportation

---

Germany during his lifetime.

7. Hermann Wilhelm Göring (1893–1946) was the most powerful leader of the Nazi party and government next to Hitler, although he lost some of his influence toward the end of the Nazi regime. He commanded the German air force during World War II and became senior commander of all armed forces. He was also given responsibility to organize all economic activity in support of the war effort.

8. The Winterhilfswerk was an annual fund drive whose collections were to be used to assist needy German citizens during the Nazi period.

9. Blessed Bernhard Lichtenberg (1875–1943) was a Roman Catholic priest who served as the provost of the St. Hedwig Cathedral in Berlin after 1932. He courageously protested the atrocities of the Nazi regime, including the treatment of Jews. Because of his activities, he was arrested and sent to a concentration camp while already seriously ill. He never reached Dachau because of his illness and was returned to Berlin for burial by the police of Hof, Germany before the Gestapo could interfere. He was declared blessed by Pope John Paul II (1920–2005) on June 23, 1996.

10. Am Fuchspass is a street in Berlin-Zehlendorf.

11. Kristallnacht, the Night of Broken Glass, occurred on November 9–10, 1938. Jewish homes, synagogues, schools, hospitals, and business establishments were destroyed by mobs of people throughout Germany and Austria. Kristallnacht marked the beginning of the public and systematic persecution of Jews in Nazi Germany. This pogrom continues to be commemorated by religious communities to this day with the hope of fostering repentance and the struggle against anti-Semitism and racism of every sort.

12. Jochen Klepper (1903–1942) was a German journalist and writer who was unable to pursue his journalistic career because of his marriage to Johanna Stein, a Jewish woman. He was drafted and served in the German army for a time. He was the son of a Lutheran pastor, and his books reflect his Christian identity. So do the hymns that he wrote. Although his wife was baptized, the family continued to experience discrimination, which led to their suicide.

to an extermination camp the next morning. Jochen Klepper's novel *The Father*, about the Prussian soldier-king,[13] had still been published in 1937. He pictured the ruler as father in the novel. The image was surely intended as an opposing model to the figure of the Führer and was also recognized as such by the Nazis.

In December 1938 Hitler established the "cross of honor for the German mother." A German mother was honored with it after her fourth child. Mother Kühn (like Mother Hartmann in Burgörner) declined being honored with the cross publicly.

The female dog Minka also belonged to the teacher's residence on the Fuchspass for several years. She liked to bring her puppies into the world on a soft feather bed. However, other "outrageous" stories about her must be recounted in another context.

---

13. Klepper, *Der Vater*. King Frederick Wilhelm I (1688–1740) was King of Prussia and Elector of Brandenburg from 1713 until 1740. He was also the father of King Frederick II (1712–1786), better known as Frederick the Great, who ruled Prussia from 1740 until 1786.

1936

Nappian and Neucke

WE GREW UP WITH biblical stories, the fairy tales of the brothers Grimm, and the story of Nappian and Neucke.[1] Each time that we traveled to the farm of our great-grandfather in Hettstedt with our parents we could see the miners Nappian and Neucke, in a lying position with tools in their hands, hewn into two stone pillars under the large industrial bridge. Our father told us, "In the past the mine shafts in this place were so narrow and flat that the miners had to work while lying down. In order not to tear the seats of their pants constantly on the stones, they wore leather protectors over the back of their pants. On the other hand, the foundry workers wore a leather apron in order to protect themselves in the front from the hot fire of the smelters in the foundries. Therefore, during festivals the miners still wear their leather protectors on the back of their pants and the foundry workers their leather aprons in front." He indeed had to know this because his father, our grandfather, had worked in the underground shaft as a supervisor. Unfortunately, he had already died before we were born.

The farm of our great-grandfather was located very near the copper mountain where Nappian and Neucke supposedly found the first copper eight hundred years ago. About that time the St. Gangolf Church was built on the copper mountain. It has been restored again in recent years. The copper mining industry of the Mansfeld region expanded from the copper mountain in Hettstedt, to the benefit and blessing of the populace. The

---

1. The story of Nappian and Neucke is a German folk tale related to the copper mining industry in the Hettstedt region.

motto, "With God there is advice and help," is embossed on the Mansfeld commemorative thaler, which was last minted in May 1915. The picture that is engraved on the coin is the knight George fighting with the dragon.

When one drives from Hettstedt to Eisleben, one can discover that there are many small hills surrounding Hettstedt. In this region the layer of copper lay immediately below the surface of the ground. The hills become larger near Burgörner, because one had to dig deeper for the layer of copper. Pyramids of shaft residue[2] rise upwards around Eisleben. Finally, near Sangerhausen one had to reach one thousand meters into the ground in order to mine a layer of copper fifteen centimeters thick. This could no longer be justified economically after the reunification of Germany (1990). All mining shafts in the Mansfeld region were shut down, and the industry related to mining died immediately with the closing. This constituted an economic collapse from which the whole region has not yet been able to recover. It is even now a human tragedy for many families. The parents belong to the long-term unemployed and the children to the youth who have no prospects.

Such a development could not be imagined during our childhood. There was work in full swing everywhere. It was rush hour on the streets during the shift changes at 6 a.m., 2 p.m., and 10 p.m. Railroads and buses transported workers to the factories. Conveyors facilitated the removal of material all the way to the top of the pyramids. The glowing slag from the foundries was transported by special lorry trains to specific slag waste dumps and emptied there. It flowed down like glowing lava streams and solidified. This could be observed particularly well in the dark. We discovered trenches in the Edward slope of shafts near Burgörner that the revolutionary, Max Hölz,[3] had built together with the rebellious workers in 1923. Max Hölz stole money from banks, landowners, and industrialists and distributed it among the poor. If someone cannot pay a bill immediately, it is said in the Mansfeld region even today, "Max Hölz will surely pay it!"

---

2. The original reads Schachtpyramiden.

3. Max Hölz (1889–1933) was a leader of the communist worker movement in Germany and became involved in armed actions that resulted in his arrest and imprisonment.

1937

My Esteemed Uncle Karl

WHEN I FIRST HEARD something about the Frankish Emperor Charlemagne in school I raised my hand and explained that our family descended from this Emperor. The teacher asked quite amazed, "Why do you believe this?" I recounted the story of my Uncle Karl, who had employed many women and men on the domain of Voldagsen in the Braunschweig region. They worked on his estate and admired him very much. I concluded, "I envision Emperor Charlemagne like my Uncle Karl. Therefore, we must, indeed, be related to him." My logic caused the gracious teacher to smile patiently, and he said, "Ultimately all of our ancestors did once belong to some Germanic tribe, to the Franks or Saxons or Thuringians or Bavarians."

Who, then, was this Uncle Karl? He was the youngest brother of my great-grandfather and managed the large domain Voldagsen since 1915. Together with my sister Irmgard I experienced beautiful weeks on this estate during the summer of 1937. I remember a huge estate, perhaps ten times as large as my great-grandfather's farm. The large courtyard was surrounded by large stables for horses, cows, sheep, pigs, and for whatever species of fowl one can imagine; expansive barns and storerooms; sheds for cars, tractors, and equipment; and, finally, a nursery with many greenhouses. The courtyard was always swept clean after work. The many carriages stood in rank and file next to each other.

The manor house, where Uncle Karl and Aunt Minna lived, was located on a narrow part of the estate and was surrounded by a small park.

We vacationing children were also housed there. A small stream bubbled along the veranda. During a storm it swelled into a raging river.

Uncle Karl sometimes took us along on his inspection drives. A French driver, who was a former prisoner of war from World War I, drove us in a black passenger car to the fields and meadows, to the fruit plantations, and into the woods that were part of the estate. We exited the car periodically. Uncle Karl greeted his employees and discussed the coming tasks with those in charge. Uncle Karl was greeted respectfully and in a friendly manner everywhere. The summer days were exceptionally hot. Uncle Karl experienced one sweat attack after another. He had supplied himself sufficiently with handkerchiefs and hung the wet handkerchiefs on his belt so that they would dry. That must certainly have been an impressive picture. The tall, dignified uncle walked through the fields and meadows with large steps and waving handkerchiefs. The little children, with whom he always joked, accompanied him on his left and right. We witnessed once when he was furious. He had discovered in the forest that traffickers had once again chopped the tops off the beautiful, slender pine trees. He instructed the estate manager to notify the police immediately. When the little stream near the veranda swelled up after a thunderstorm and washed ashore parts of collapsed barns and houses, kitchen utensils, furniture, and drowned cattle, Uncle Karl immediately organized a cadre of helpers who initiated the necessary steps in the neighborhood, together with the fire department. We were genuinely proud of our Uncle Karl.

1938

A Jewish Store Destroyed

I REMEMBER NOVEMBER 10, 1938[1] very well. My mother had been in Hettstedt with Irmgard in order to do some shopping. They returned completely distraught. They had witnessed how citizens of Hettstedt destroyed the department store Schön on the market place and threw the furnishings of the Jewish merchant, Schön, out of the window. Tables, chairs, cupboards, armchairs, and sofas—even a piano was among the furnishings. Everything shattered into a thousand pieces in the midst of the loud howling of a stirred up crowd.

During the previous night most of the synagogues in all of Germany were set on fire. The little synagogue in Eisleben, to whose congregation the few Hettstedt Jews belonged, was so integrated into the other buildings of the Lutherstrasse that the whole street would have burned down with it if it had been set ablaze. However, the inside of the synagogue was destroyed, as well as the Jewish stores on the market places of Eisleben and Hettstedt.

We children initially became aware of the "Jewish problem" through the occurrences of November 9 and 10, 1938. We reacted with fright and helplessness. Our mother certainly included the affected Jewish families in the evening prayer. At some point during the war the so-called "little man" appeared among us twice, each time for fourteen days. We saw him only during mealtimes. He sat at table with us as a guest. He looked sick and miserable. His large eyes sometimes stared at us: to question? to examine? He was a mystery to us. Our parents had told us nothing about him. They

---

1. See footnote 11 in chapter 1935.

asked us to be kind to the poor man. They also commanded us strictly to tell no one, including a fellow schoolmate, about this "little man."

When praying the prayer at the noon meal, "Come, Lord Jesus, be our guest . . ." I sometimes posed the question, but only to myself: "Does Jesus have anything to do with this 'little man' at our table?" After fourteen days the "little man" disappeared as surprisingly as he had arrived.

It must also have been about this time that I heard something about "Buchenwald" for the first time. Our mailman often left packages in our entrance hall for a few hours that he later distributed in the upper village. We inquisitive children spelled out the addresses of the senders and recipients on the packages and made up a variety of fantastic stories. One day I discovered the beautiful place name "Buchenwald"[2] in the address of the sender. I asked my mother where this village with the beautiful name was. My mother turned pale and stammered: "Let us not speak about this terrible place." I did not inquire further. Soon after the end of the war I read Wiechert's *Totenwald* and always thought about the frightened face of my mother while doing so. After all, she knew even before the war that "Buchenwald" was a terrible Totenwald. The Evangelical pastor Schneider[3] was murdered in this concentration camp already in 1938.

---

2. Buchenwald literally means "beech tree forest."

3. Paul Schneider (1897–1939) was an Evangelical pastor who is often referred to as the "preacher of Buchenwald." When the National Socialists came to power, he concluded that their policies contradicted the teachings of Scripture. He therefore joined the Confessing Church and opposed the efforts of the Nazis to interfere in ecclesiastical matters. In 1937 he was arrested and imprisoned in the Buchenwald concentration camp. He continued to be a faithful witness in the camp, was forced to do hard labor, was often beaten and tortured because of his defiance of the Nazis, and was eventually murdered. Dietrich Bonhoeffer (1906–1945) considered Schneider to be the first martyr of the Confessing Church. Schneider's courageous witness is recognized by both Protestant communities and by the Roman Catholic Church, and a candle continues to be lit in his former cell in Buchenwald. His wife, Margarete Dietrich Schneider (1904–2002) and their six children survived him. Margarete Schneider was actively involved in the ministry to women in the Evangelical Church in Württemberg after World War II.

1939

Vacation in Trockenborn

In the summer of 1939 our parents traveled with us four children to Trockenborn, close to Leuchtenburg Castle near Kahla. Our mother's oldest sister lived in the Trockenborn parsonage with her husband and three children.

We vacation guests were housed in the so-called "old fortress," directly above the chicken coop. When the rooster crowed early in the morning, we almost fell out of our beds. However, we also wanted to rise as early as possible because there was so much to experience! This began right away with the visit to the toilet. The toilet, a so-called "dry toilet," was located at the end of a long hallway in the parsonage. It was occupied most of the time because there were so many people. However, there were also other reasons for this reality. The walls of the toilet were decorated with genuinely funny drawings, cut out of the comics sections of newspapers. One needed time to view all of them. A peal of laughter rang through the hallway every time a person sitting on the "throne" understood a joke.

A sawmill was located very near the parsonage. We could watch for hours as boards were created out of the huge tree trunks. The smell of fresh wood was wonderful.

We also befriended a number of "cow farmers." They could not afford horses. They yoked milk cows to their wagons. They did, of course, have all the other animals that belong to a farm: pigs, sheep, geese, ducks, and chickens.

The Quest for Faithfulness

However, the moated castle Fröhliche Wiederkunft, where a genuine duke lived, was the biggest attraction for us children in Trockenborn. The duke drove through the village periodically with a carriage. He had no political power since 1918. Of the many castles in the former duchy of Sachsen-Altenburg that he had owned, he could retain only this one. During the sixteenth century, Duke John Frederick[1] reunited with his wife in the castle Fröhliche Wiederkunft after he was released from the imprisonment of the emperor. Therefore, the castle was given this name, "Joyous Return."

We children also sensed something about the imminent beginning of the war that occurred in September 1939. During the last days of vacation, the Kärner brothers, cousins of my mother, met in Trockenborn together with their wives. The oldest brother was at that time on his honeymoon trip throughout Germany. He was no longer allowed to return to his pharmacy in Chile so close to the war's beginning. Every "ethnic German" was now needed in Germany—that is what one could read in the newspapers, and so it was announced in the "people's radio."[2]

We children did not participate in the conversations of the adults. However, as we said goodbye to each other there were many tears, also on the part of the adults. After all, the men all had to assume that they would be drafted. We began to suspect that war can become very horrible.

---

1. Duke John Frederick of Saxony (1503–1554) was a Lutheran prince and one of the leaders of the Schmalkaldic League, a defensive alliance of the Lutheran political entities during the sixteenth century. When Emperor Charles V (1500–1558) initiated military action against the Schmalkaldic League, the then Elector John Frederick was captured and imprisoned. He was also stripped of his electoral title. The reunion with his spouse Sybille of Cleves (1512–1554) and their family, to which Hartmann is referring, occurred at the Wolfersdorf Castle. John Frederick renamed it after this joyous event.

2. The Volksempfänger or "people's radio," officially named VE 301, was a radio that was manufactured by various companies and was supposed to be reasonably priced so that people could afford to purchase it. The Nazi government broadcast its propaganda over the Volksempfänger.

1940

Birthdays, Hamsters, and May Beetles

ONE YEAR AFTER MY enrollment in the Hüttenschule—an Easter bunny peeked out of my sugar cone[1] because we started school after Easter vacation—war broke out. We knew from the beginning that war was something horrible, but we did not yet experience any effects of war during the first two years. The new boy and girl friends that we made in school came to our house to play most of the time because we had more room in the house and garden. However, because of the birthdays of the children we also visited the small village homes. The parlor was opened for the birthday celebrations. Otherwise it was used only for special festivals. Normal family life occurred in a very small kitchen or in the slightly larger laundry room in the annex, in which a granular coke oven provided even heat and constantly hot water. Fruit-topped cake with a gold-yellow layer made of milk, pudding, eggs, and sugar that was unfamiliar to us at home was served during the children's birthday celebrations in the parlor. Gelatin[2] in red or yellow was also unknown to us until then. On the other hand, the village children enjoyed the chocolate cake that only my mother could bake.

My friend Werner Conrad had an older brother who went to dig for hamsters in the stubble fields during the summer after the harvest. Werner

---

1. The Zuckertüte or Schultüte is a cone-shaped paper, cardboard, or plastic container filled with various candies and treats. German children receive it as a traditional present on their first day of elementary school.

2. Hartmann uses the term Zitterpudding.

and I were quite proud that the big brother took us along. In return, we gladly carried the spade; an empty sack; and a long, flexible wire. First, the hamster den was inspected for evidence of current use. When there were small footprints or traces of fresh earth or several ears of grain at the entrance, the digging could begin. One had to proceed quite carefully. After every insertion of the spade the continuing direction of the entrance passage was examined with the assistance of the wire. For safety reasons the hamster built curves and corners into the underground passages, sometimes to the right, sometimes to the left, sometimes straight ahead, but always deeper into the ground. The destination of the digging was the "dining room" of the hamster family. Sometimes one found there a half centner[3] of grain. With this amount of grain the Conrad family could feed its chickens for several months. It was always exciting to see whether we would meet the residents of the subterranean structure during these excavations. Normally, the hamster family flees through a back exit when it hears suspicious noises near the main entrance. However, we also experienced the Betze, or hamster mother, jumping toward us, ready to attack. She feared for her young. Werner's brother warded her off with the spade. Sometimes it was a fatal blow.

In May and June we occupied ourselves with the May beetles. The first ones were carefully collected into cigar boxes whose lids were punctured in order to allow air intake. Some years the May beetles became a nuisance. We built instruments that consisted of a stick and the lid of a box with which to strike the May beetles and went with the instruments to a bare hill, the so-called Brache, in the evening. The May beetles, by the hundreds of thousands, flew low over the ground there. We slapped them to the ground, stepped on them, and shoveled them into sacks. Dead May beetles are supposedly good food for chickens and promote egg production. A horrible story. Were we not already in the midst of war?

"Fly, May beetle. The father is in the war. The mother is in Pomerania. Pomerania has burned. Fly, May beetle."[4]

---

3. A centner is a unit of weight in European countries of 50 kilograms or about 110 pounds.

4. Hartmann is quoting the lyrics of a well-known folk and children's song. Its origins are uncertain, but various versions of the song have been printed since the early nineteenth century.

1941

Expatriates in Our Village

POLES HAD COME TO our village as seasonal workers during the harvest season already before the war. They lived very near to us on the estate. They were fond of children and joked with us.

After the beginning of the war the Poles came as prisoners of war or as conscripted laborers, among them many women. They were distributed among large estates and among small farms and nurseries. Initially, their behavior toward the German population was very unfriendly and cold. The captured soldiers were proud and at the same time bitter because of the lost war. They were concerned about their families and their country. However, gradually the relations between us became more humane. The Poles' freedom to move about increased. Poles from the whole region met every Sunday morning for worship in Polish in the Roman Catholic church. On Sunday afternoon they went for walks together or enjoyed each other's company in their lodgings.

Other prisoners came to the Mansfeld territory beginning in 1940: French, Netherlanders, Belgians, English, and Serbs. They worked in the foundries and factories or in the copper shafts. After the invasion of the Soviet Union, Russian prisoners and conscripted workers from the Ukraine and Belarus were added. They were initially housed in isolation from the German citizenry. Our village residents were horrified by their appearance when they traveled through our village on the way to work and during the return to the camp. They were emaciated, clothed in rags, with wooden clogs, often without stockings even in the winter. We did not regard them with contempt but felt sorry for them as unfortunate people. Even we children ascertained that prisoners from all other countries were treated better than the Russians.

A Ukrainian farmer was appointed "milker"[1] for the cow barn on the manor. He lived with his wife and two small children in the "milker house." The children were initially very shy. However, as they noticed that German children can also be friendly, they became more trusting. Although it was officially forbidden, our mother began to provide clothing for the children. As we played together on the manor, we put hats, coats, and jackets on the Ukrainian children. We also heard that some German workers shared their breakfast or snack with Russians and Ukrainians.

When captured Indians with authentic turbans[2] marched through our streets one day, it was a sensation in our village. They had fought on the side of the British. They were housed for several weeks in the large hall of the Restaurant Wagner. We could observe through the large windows how the Indians rolled and unrolled their turbans. They could not cope with the difficult work in the copper shafts. Therefore, they were transferred elsewhere.

In April 1945 the area around Hettstedt was for several days without any law enforcement agency. The German law enforcers had fled, and the American occupying authorities had not yet been installed. Several thousand prisoners of war had suddenly been freed in our region. Chaos threatened. Some French, Belgian, Serb, and English prisoners took the initiative at that time. They saw to it that there was peace and order until the Americans appointed a military command in Hettstedt.

---

1. The term Schweizer was used to describe people who worked in the dairy industry and performed various tasks, including the tending and milking of the cows.

2. These prisoners of war were likely Sikhs or Punjabis.

1942

We Visit Our Great-grandfather

LIKE ALL CHILDREN, WE had two grandfathers. The one, the miner and supervisor Wilhelm Hartmann from Hettstedt, had already died before I was born. The other, the Pastor Franz Burger, had died in 1938 in Kahla, Thuringia. We met him only a few times, and he was already very sick at that time. However, we had a great-grandfather on account of whom all my classmates were envious of me. He died at the age of 92 in the year 1947. He owned a stately farm in Hettstedt.

When we wanted to visit our great-grandfather, we had to walk three kilometers. However, that was no problem for us since we experienced so many interesting things on the way. On the street past the lead refinery we watched how glowing clumps of slag were dumped on a courtyard and broken up into small pieces with large hammers. We passed very large chimneys. Small factory trains passed by us. Long trains traveled high above us over a cement bridge with many arches. This bridge had been constructed by Italian prisoners during World War I. A large black cross was a reminder that there were also fatal accidents as the bridge was built.

In Neudorf we passed the Gasthof zum Grafen Waldersee. We told each other terrible, gory stories about this count. Did he not participate in the suppression of the Boxer Rebellion[1] in China? We stopped at the new movie theater and wanted to know which coming fairy-tale movies were advertised.

1. The Boxer Rebellion occurred between 1898 and 1901 and was an armed revolt by a nationalistic militia movement that sought to free China from European colonialism and from Christian missionary presence and activities.

In Hettstedt we had to make a decision. We sometimes ascended a steep path to the Elisenhöhe. Most of the time we then greeted the friendly, stout midwife in her small house. She had helped us four siblings come into the world healthy and happy. From the Elisenhöhe we arrived at the Himmelshöhe, ran around our great-grandfather's farm on a narrow lane, and arrived at the crossing of two attractive streets with the lovely names Rosenkränzchen I and Rosenkränzchen II. From this crossing we entered the farm.

Alternatively, we continued on the lower street for a few hundred meters more; passed by a large dairy behind the post office; ran across the Augustusplatz, past the workshop of the tailor Raspe; and turned into the Hohestrasse. Shortly before the Hoffman Bakery a narrow slipway led directly to the farm by means of a steep stairway. We immediately detected our great-grandfather. He sat on an easy chair near the window and waited for us. We stormed across the courtyard and entered the house through an unusual door. It consisted of two parts, an upper and lower one, and during the summer the upper door was always open. Great-grandfather fed the chickens and geese as well as the mother hens and their chicks from this door. They all came running when he called them: "Hum, put, put, put, hum, hum, hum . . . !" Great-grandfather always had something prepared for us as a welcome when we came to visit. Each of us received a pear or an apple or a few cherries. After our long journey, all of us, of course, had to go to the toilet first. That was a very special experience on the farm. Two little houses with heart-shaped openings in the doors and in the stone walls were located adjacent to the manure pile. Our "transactions," whether big or small, fell directly onto the manure pile through a large hole.

After the visit to the toilet, coffee and cake were provided, on Sundays most of the time in the parlor. Cake with crumble topping, sugar cake, or a cake topped with fruit were offered, all homemade. The parlor was interesting. When one entered through the door, an old, beautiful cabinet was located to the left. There were marvelous things in the cabinet: a box of toy bricks with which one could build houses and fortresses. At home we had only wooden building blocks. There was also a large doll with leg and arm joints and with real hair. We constantly dressed and undressed the doll in order to admire her joints. To the right of the entrance door one could see a sofa and in the corner also a comfortable chair. A pendulum clock ticked above the chair. Then one came to a cozy stove, before which the dog, who was already old, lay most of the time. Next to the stove, a door led to

We Visit Our Great-grandfather

the bedroom of our great-grandfather. Our great-grandmother had passed away long ago. We did not know her. Across from the entrance door, two armchairs were located near the two windows of the living room. The one was reserved for our great-grandfather. The fourth wall was occupied by a large, flat clavichord. It served as the repository for pictures and books. Our deceased great-grandmother presumably had still played the clavichord.

In the middle of the square room stood a table that could be extended on both sides when company was present. An old vaulted ceiling spanned the whole room, which gave it a dignified coziness. We experienced family celebrations, both for happy and sad occasions, in this room.

Our great-grandfather wore his hat also in the room. It was a kind of a sailor's cap, though not dark gray but a light green gray. He could wonderfully tell stories about his childhood and about his poor, blind king[2] whom the Prussians had driven out of Hanover. He also recounted for us how Prussian hussars[3] came during a war and senselessly trampled a ripe grain field that belonged to his father. Our great-grandfather was born in Lower Saxony in 1854. He emigrated to Hettstedt with his young wife and established a new farm there.

When we visited our great-grandfather we, of course, went into the stables, romped through the barns, helped with the feeding, and looked for eggs that were hidden. However, I have recounted this in another place.

---

2. The great-grandfather was referring to King George V (1819–1878), who was the last king of Hanover.

3. Hussars were light cavalry soldiers.

1943

Berlin Evacuation

WHEN WE TRAVEL BY train from Dessau to Hettstedt in order to care for the grave of my parents and to visit our Hettstedt relatives, we always have to change trains in Güsten. The train station, which is now deserted, has no ticket counter, no waiting room, and no toilet. It does have decayed, long hallways; empty staircases; and unused large buildings, and it dreams about old times. Güsten was once an important rail hub for passenger and freight traffic on the Berlin–Kassel line, the so-called "cannons railway" constructed after the Franco-Prussian War of 1870 to 1871.

Christiane still remembers very precisely a hot August day in the year 1943 in the Güsten train station. Her parents with the five children and grandmother Koepke had hurriedly left Berlin. By means of a mailed general announcement on August 1, the propaganda minister Joseph Goebbels[1] had exhorted the Berlin residents to go to regions of the Reich[2] that were less in danger of an airstrike. The evacuation notification was addressed to women, children, people of independent means, retirees,

---

1. Joseph Goebbels (1897–1945) was a close friend and supporter of Adolf Hitler and served as Minister of Propaganda in Nazi Germany from 1933 until 1945. As such, he strictly controlled all the news media and publications in Germany. He was an ardent anti–Semite and advocated for the extermination of the Jews. He also opposed Christianity and the church. According to Hitler's wishes, he succeeded Hitler as Chancellor of Germany, but only for one day. He and his wife committed suicide after poisoning their children.

2. The Nazis and their supporters referred to Germany as the Deutsche Reich, the German Empire; the Dritte Reich, the Third Empire; or simply the Reich, the Empire.

and other residents who were not bound to Berlin because of vocational or other reasons. Many Berlin families were startled while having Sunday morning coffee. Seven hundred thousand Berlin residents left the city by the end of 1943.

The departure of the Kühn family must have occurred at the beginning of August. The children sweated under their winter clothing and with the large amount of carry-on luggage. The train station in Güsten, where one had to transfer trains, was prepared for the streams of evacuees. Friendly Sisters of the German Red Cross cared for the children. They were offered food and drink in the waiting rooms. Gebhard was three years old at that time, Friederike was seven, Dankwart was nine, Christiane was eleven, and Berthold was thirteen. The destination of their journey was Wiehe in the Unstrut Valley. Relatives of grandmother Koepke lived there. At short notice, they had indicated that they were willing to host the large Kühn family with its eight members. How was that to be accomplished? The Kühns from Berlin as well as the hosts from Wiehe must have thought about the next weeks with concern. After an extended stay in Güsten—Christiane still recalls precisely a comely waitress with a blue apron and white collar who brought her a tasty bean soup—the family could resume their travels. The new train was overfilled, just like the Berlin train. Soldiers, evacuees, and workers from the Junkers factories[3] in Dessau and Aschersleben and from the foundries and mines in the Mansfeld territory all jostled each other in the compartments and aisles. Some even rode along on the steps of the train.

Since Wiehe has no train station, the Berliners had to disembark in Rossleben. On the train station square, a horse-drawn vehicle waited for the evacuees from the capital of the Reich. The city children climbed onto the farm wagon with interest and in good spirits. The news must have spread quickly in Wiehe and the surrounding area that the first evacuees were coming. The Berliners were examined inquisitively and critically as they drove through busy streets.

They were cordially welcomed at the Restaurant zur Tanne and invited to the evening meal, which consisted of beer soup with whipped egg white. The little Berlin children had never eaten something like this. There was great disappointment on both sides! How could it go well in the next weeks? It went well!

---

3. The Junkers factories manufactured airplane engines and airplanes.

Three months later the Kühns could move into an empty parsonage in neighboring Allerstedt to which belonged a large garden, which they could use. How long would they have to live in this impractical house, which had virtually no furniture and which was very cold in the winter? However, they had much room and the large garden! When would they be able to return to their beautiful home in Berlin-Zehlendorf? Goebbels's call for the evacuation of the Berlin inhabitants was interpreted by many people as the beginning of the end. However, how long would the end still last?

The Russian victory in the battle of Stalingrad; the courageous leaflet campaign of the "White Rose" in Munich[4] that resulted in many capital punishments; the retreat of the German troops from North Africa, which could no longer be stopped; and the landing of the allies in Sicily were all unmistakable signs of the imminent end of Nazi rule. However, the war still lasted two more years.

The Kühns lived on the parish property in Allerstedt for three years. Then they moved to Schulpforta and later to Naumburg. They did not return to Berlin. Their home on Fuchspass in Zehlendorf lay in ruins.

---

4. The members of the "White Rose" group in Munich were primarily students and professors at the University who were opposed to the Nazi regime and its policies, including the persecution of the Jews. They were also pacifists. They spread their message primarily by means of pamphlets that they distributed, especially in southern Germany. The members of the group were arrested by the Gestapo on February 19, 1943 and placed on trial. Most were either imprisoned or executed.

1944

For the Sake of Victory

WE CHILDREN IN THE parsonage already comprehended very early that the rule of the Nazis was a disaster for Germany. Nevertheless, we cheered the victories of the German armies on all fronts, like all youth of the same age. We were inspired by the holders of the knight's cross, collected their pictures, and read their biographies. We were pleased with every special report of German victories. The conflict pursued me into my personal evening prayers. I wanted German troops to be victorious throughout the world. At the same time, I hoped that the rule of the Nazis would soon cease.

However, eventually we growing children also became tired of the war. The ever increasing air raid warnings, which persisted for hours some nights, and the disheartening casualty reports of fallen fathers and sons from our village allowed doubt to begin to grow in us. The mail carrier could no longer cope with carrying casualty reports to the families. He brought them to our mother. She then assumed this difficult assignment.

When the American and British troops landed in Normandy in June 1944, it was clear to us that the war could no longer be won. The assassination attempt on July 20, 1944 in the Wolf's Lair[1] in East Prussia startled us. We followed the subsequent processes in the people's court with greatest attention and with the innermost interest. During our daily train rides to school we were met more and more frequently by trains of soldiers with

---

1. The Wolfsschanze or "Wolf's Lair" was a headquarters that Hitler used, particularly when focusing his attention on the Eastern front. It received its name because of Hitler's nickname "Wolf," which he himself adopted. A failed assassination attempt was made at this location on July 20, 1944.

the slogan on the locomotive: "Wheels must roll for the sake of victory." We students whispered into each others' ears: "Heads must roll for the sake of victory!"

A fellow student constantly carried a red star with hammer and sickle in his pants pocket. He probably exchanged it with a Russian prisoner of war for a breakfast. We viewed the star like a horoscope only when we were alone in a very small group. In the fall the refugee transports from the western border arrived among us in central Germany. Boys from Aachen suddenly sat next to us in our classes. They brought a new secret sign to our school, the Edelweiss.[2] We were not certain about this, but we suspected that the Edelweiss was something similar to the "White Rose" in Munich, a secret sign for an opposition movement. We had heard about the capital punishments in Munich. We had to deal carefully with such suspicions.

When we were dismissed for Christmas vacation it was clear to us that the war could not last much longer. The front line of the war had been pushed everywhere to the borders of the German Reich. Would now not have been the right moment for Germany to surrender? However, we surely sensed that it would be a frightful ending. There were people in our country, also in our village, who still believed in the wonder weapons, the V1 and V2[3] from Peenemünde on the Baltic Sea. We resigned ourselves to draw the following conclusion: The war will end only when all of Germany lies in rubble. We experienced the transition from the old to the new year with this somber prognosis.

---

2. The Edelweisspiraten, or the "Edelweiss Pirates," were groups of young people, typically between the ages of fourteen and seventeen, who were opposed particularly to the military nature of the German Youth Movement, the official youth organization in Nazi Germany, and who wanted to exercise more freedoms in the German society. They used the Edelweiss as their symbol. They were antagonistic to members of the German Youth Movement, even to the point of using physical violence against them. The Nazis sought to control their activities and often punished those who were arrested. After World War II some of the Edelweiss groups also opposed the policies of the Allied occupying powers and perpetrated acts of violence against Russians and Poles and against German women who befriended foreign soldiers.

3. The V1 and V2 were missiles developed by Nazi Germany and used as long-range weapons, particularly against Britain.

1945

Liberation

THIS IS THE WAY that we actually experienced the end of Nazi rule, as liberation. There were still so many dreadful occurrences during the first months of 1945. Such cities as Dessau, Zerbst, Halberstadt, or Nordhausen, to name only a few, were destroyed in a senseless manner. Low-flying aircraft attacked trains, farm wagons, and bicyclists. Courts of summary jurisdiction condemned deserters to death. There was a dogfight over our village. The German pilot burned with his plane in the middle of our village after an emergency landing. The American pilot was able to rescue himself from his burning plane with a parachute but was almost lynched by the German populace.

Suddenly our village was occupied by American troops. The centrally located parsonage was chosen as headquarters for the management of the battle. Within half an hour the pastor's family and all of the evacuees who lived with us had to leave the house. Families in the neighborhood spontaneously accommodated us. A unit of soldiers with artillery had dug in on the periphery of our village. They fired their shells all night long in the direction of the Harz, where German troops still offered resistance.

The next morning the American troops moved on. They left a Tohuwabohu[1] in our house: cured sausages, canned meat, unused laundry, and a huge number of cigarettes. And newspapers! President Roosevelt had just died. The American newspapers reported extensively about his funeral. A few days later the occupation forces arrived. They established a military

---

1. See Gen 1:2; from the Hebrew meaning "a formless void" or "formless and empty."

command in Hettstedt. "Respectable" women and men were appointed municipal leaders in the individual communities. In our village the cantor functioned as mayor for several weeks. The schools remained closed for the time being. The process of supplying food went amazingly well. The many thousand freed prisoners of war behaved in a disciplined manner, with a few exceptions.

In June rumors that alarmed us arose suddenly: the Americans are going to leave us. We will be included in the Soviet occupation zone. Particularly many refugees from the East panicked because of the rumors and set out in a westerly direction. The rumor became a reality. The American troops retreated with their perfect technical armaments. On July 1 a seemingly unending caravan moved through the empty streets of our village a few hours later. There were little wagons, pulled by koniks, that had small artillery or field kitchens coupled to them. On the wagons were young soldiers in shabby uniforms, friendly and gazing with amazement. Some sang or played merry or melancholy songs on accordions. The residents of the village gradually appeared on the streets. Germans and Russians smiled at and greeted each other cheerfully. All took a deep breath. The war had ended. Hatred, revenge, retaliation, fear, and mistrust no longer existed. The war had ended! Everything must certainly be fine now!

However, that did not happen quickly. We read with horror in the newspapers about the atrocities in the concentration camps and about the unimaginable consequences of the two atomic bombs dropped on Japan. How should all of this be processed? Was it conceivable that there would be independent international courts that could sentence those who were chiefly responsible?

New hostile stances already emerged. The East-West conflict began already a few weeks after the end of the war. A land reform was implemented in the Soviet occupation zone in the fall of 1945 that was not discussed with the Western zones. Our population was open to a land reform with the hope that many resettled farmers from the East could build up a new livelihood by this means. However, many people were disappointed that the landowners were dispossessed without compensation and could not continue an agricultural business under four hundred morgen[2] and that injustice and arbitrariness were associated with the dispossessions.

---

2. A varying land measurement that equates to 0.6 to 0.9 acres, depending on the region.

Liberation

We experienced such injustice in close proximity. A tenant farmer lived on our estate. The estate was owned by the Mansfeld factories. The tenant farmer was treated like a big landowner. Around 7 p.m. he was told that he and his family had to leave the Mansfeld hill region by 11 p.m. Our mother, my older sister, and I helped the disconcerted family to remain calm and to distinguish between the important and unimportant possessions. They were permitted to load one horse-drawn wagon. A control group came every hour. Its members went arrogantly and contemptuously through all the rooms, simply to indicate that they were now the lords. We hid in a closet each time they came. No one was permitted to help the farm family. Because the curfew began at 11 p.m. the prescribed time for departure was extended to 5 a.m. We accompanied the expelled family to the exit of the village before the village awakened.

These and other experiences at the end of the year of liberation troubled us. How would a new democratic life develop? The first steps of newly established parties were very restricted. The Social Democrats, who openly manifested that they opposed unification with the Communist Party of Germany, were harassed. The first people already began to leave for the West.

During the winter of 1945 to 1946 a wave of arrests spread through our zone. People in commerce and scientists, with or without a Nazi past, were arrested during the night. The director of the foundry was arrested by Soviet officials in the villa next door to us one late evening. This was done noisily and forcefully. We were frightened but could not help. His wife and the two young girls, friends of my sisters, never heard anything about their father again.

In the fall of 1945 instruction began again in the school in Aschersleben with a new director, with very many new teachers and many new students, and with endless difficulties. There were no textbooks. The trains, like the classrooms,[3] were not heated during the winter. However, we did not allow ourselves to be discouraged!

---

3. The original reads Schulklassen, which means classes or grades. However, the context suggests that Hartmann meant to write Klassenzimmer, which means "classrooms."

1946

The 400th Anniversary of Martin Luther's Death

OUR PARENTS WALKED THIRTEEN kilometers with us children from Burgörner near Hettstedt to Eisleben. No buses ran at that time. The festival worship service on the occasion of the quadricentennial anniversary of Luther's death in the St. Andrew Church in Eisleben was for us children the first larger, inter-parish ecclesiastical event. Such events did not occur during the war, and before the war we children were still too small. Our parents were glad to be reunited with acquaintances from the time of the church struggle.[1] However, they also wanted to hear news about the reconstruction of the ecclesiastical organization. A new ecclesiastical leadership was supposed to be installed in Magdeburg during the following weeks. Otto Dibelius,[2] who was announced as preacher for the worship service, was slated to become bishop in Berlin. This much we children did understand.

---

1. Hartmann is referring to the church struggle or Kirchenkampf carried on between 1933 and 1945 by Christians opposed to Hitler and Nazi policies, also with regard to the church.

2. Friedrich Karl Otto Dibelius (1880–1967), generally known as Otto Dibelius, was an Evangelical pastor who served several congregations in northern Germany and Berlin before functioning as general superintendent of Brandenburg from 1925 until 1933. During this time he also joined the German National People's Party, which was both nationalistic and anti-Semitic. At the same time, he envisioned the Christian church as the defender of Christian culture in the West. Although he had agreed with Nazi anti-Semitism, he opposed Nazi efforts to control the church by means of the German Christian movement and joined the Confessing Church. After World War II, Dibelius became

The 400th Anniversary of Martin Luther's Death

Some months previously, dramatic scenes still occurred on the road that we traveled. The last unit of German troops that we had seen consisted of sixteen-year-old youngsters in uniforms of the labor service.[3] They were still convinced that they could stop the advance of the Americans. A few days later American troops controlled the street with the most current war technology. In the meantime, endless processions of refugees, people with farm wagons, bicycles, strollers, and handcarts; freed prisoners; and foreign workers from all nations moved along the road. All somehow wanted to continue on, some back home. Many no longer had a home. Again, some months later the Soviet army traversed this road with little horses and one-horse carts. We children did not know what all of this meant politically. For us it was important that there were no more bombing attacks and that the war was over. School had begun again. We looked to the future with much curiosity.

The road to Eisleben led past many pyramids of mining debris. They are small near Hettstedt, and some of these originated during the time of Luther. The nearer we came to Eisleben, the larger they became. Some of the pointed cones are higher than the pyramid of Cheops in Egypt. We had known since we were little that Luther's father, like our grandfather, was a miner. We were often in Luther's parents' home in Mansfeld, which was five kilometers from our village. We were also often in the Mansfeld Castle, whose lord was Baron von der Recke, a courageous friend of the Confessing Church. Large paintings with scenes from Luther's life hung in our village church: Luther at the Diet of Worms; Luther translating the Bible; Luther in the circle of his family. We also knew that Luther was born and also died in Eisleben. However, we had not yet visited the Luther sites in Eisleben.

I once visited a doctor in Eisleben with my mother during the war. As we went to the bus station during dusk several timid women with a yellow Star of David on their coats met us. They had prescribed times for shopping. My mother was deeply moved. She was unable to say a word. I also

---

a member of the Christian Democratic Union party and was also elected bishop of the Evangelical Church in Berlin-Brandenburg in 1948. Because he opposed communism and the East German regime, he was forbidden to enter East Berlin and the German Democratic Republic. His ecclesiastical service also included the role of chairperson of the Council of the Evangelical Church in Germany and the part-time presidency of the World Council of Churches.

3. The Arbeitsdienst, more precisely the Reichsarbeitsdienst, was compulsory service that young men had to perform in Nazi Germany before they began their Wehrdienst or military service. During World War II, young women also had to perform this mandatory labor service. Both women and men were required to wear a brown uniform.

did not ask. I had understood that the women with the star were in much trouble, and our mother did not know how to help them. That had to be in the year 1941.

On February 18, 1946 I knew more. As we entered the St. Andrew Church in Eisleben on that day, many people had already gathered. We still found seating in one of the side aisles. I do not know anymore whether the church was heated or whether it was ice cold. For me the filled church with so many people full of expectation was the grand experience. People who recognized each other waved to each other or fell into each other's arms. My parents were greeted warmly by the local Pastor Galle, a small, dignified man with a white goatee. My mother whispered to me: "Four of his sons were killed during the war!" My father waved to a Mrs. Fleischhack. Her husband, who later became provost of Magdeburg, was still a Russian prisoner of war. He only returned to his St. Andrew congregation in 1949. The congregation had to wait for its second pastor for eight years. During the worship service I was impressed by the organ music, the communal singing of the large congregation, and the close attention of the visitors during the sermon of Otto Dibelius. All expected that something new had to happen in the church. I discovered much later, when I served as pastor of the St. Andrew Church, what the ecclesiastical situation was in Eisleben at the end of the war.

There was a pastor at the St. Peter's Church who blessed his confirmands in the uniforms of the Hitler Youth and the League of German Girls. A Pastor Noack served in the St. Ann Church. He was imprisoned because he listened to foreign radio stations. A German Christian superintendent served in the St. Nicholas Church. The two pastors of the St. Andrew Church belonged to the Confessing Church. What differences there were in the Evangelical congregations of a small town of 20,000 inhabitants!

I do not know whether Otto Dibelius commented on the last sermon of Martin Luther, which he delivered in the St. Andrew Church on February 15, 1546 on Matthew 11:25–30. As I read twenty years later, in the sermon Luther warns the clever and the wise, the electors and the pastors, that they desire to be wiser than Christ. Luther's last sermon ends with the words: "Christ calls us in the friendliest manner to say, 'You are my dear Lord and Master. I am your student.' This and much more should be said about this gospel, but I am too weak. We want to leave it here."[4] After his attack of fatigue Luther gathered himself up one more time and spoke threaten-

---

4. See WA 51, 194. See also LW 53, 392.

ing words against the Jews: "If the Jews are willing to convert to us and stop their blasphemy and whatever else they have done to us, we will gladly forgive them. However, if they are not, we shall also not tolerate or endure them among us."[5] Those are Luther's last words spoken in public that cannot really be brought into harmony with his last sermon. Perhaps the old Countess Dorothee von Solms[6] already recognized this when, shortly after Luther's death, she prevented the expulsion of the Jews from the county of Mansfeld that Count Albrecht[7] planned. About four hundred Jews lived at that time outside the gates of Eisleben in Unterrissdorf, among them many refugees from Halle and Magdeburg.

Was the theme "the Jews" brought up at all on February 18, 1946? I do not know. None of the eighty Jews who were still in Eisleben in 1938 lived in this city in 1946. They were either still able to flee, or they were murdered in Theresienstadt[8] in the years 1943 and 1944. When we wanted to address this theme in Eisleben twenty-two years later, namely, in 1968, we bumped up against strong opposition in the ecclesiastical circles, among the population, and also on the part of the governmental agencies.

Soon after the service we left for home. We passed the Lenin monument that had been erected six months earlier a few hundred meters away from the Luther monument. A new challenge was looming regarding whose proportions I still surmised nothing as a fourteen-year-old. (The Lenin monument can now be seen in the armory in Berlin.)

As I imagine the return from Eisleben to Burgörner, which was again a thirteen-kilometer walk, now, fifty years later, I must register the following. All the mining shafts in the Mansfeld region have been shut down. The foundries near Helbra and Hettstedt are no longer in service. Unemployment in the region is particularly high. The devastating effects of a long-term unemployment are becoming noticeable. We must hope that

---

5. WA 51, 196. This section is not included in the translation of the sermon in LW.

6. Countess Dorothea of Mansfeld (1493–1578) was the daughter of Count Philip of Solms-Lich (1468–1544) and Adriane of Hanau-Münzenberg, Countess of Solms-Lich (1468–1524). She became the Countess of Mansfeld when she married Count Ernst II of Mansfeld-Vorderort (1479–1531) and is particularly known for her medical knowledge and her healing practices. Even Martin Luther sought her medical advice. Her support of the Jewish community in the region is historically noteworthy.

7. Count Albrecht VII of Mansfeld-Hinterort (1480–1560) affirmed the Lutheran reform movement, signed the Augsburg Confession, and joined the Schmalkaldic League.

8. Theresienstadt was a concentration camp in the Czech city of Terezin, which was under German occupation during World War II.

the Luther anniversary offers more than the promotion of tourism and the marketing of the Reformer.

I witnessed the four-hundred-fiftieth anniversary of Luther's death in Eisleben as a retired person. I experienced myself to be a listener full of expectation to whom Martin Luther addresses this wish in his last sermon: "I do not believe in my pastor. Rather, he tells me about another Lord who is called Christ . . . [He is] the true master and teacher."[9] I await direction for our church from Him in view of the new challenges presented by a "social market economy" that lets the social components shrink more and more.

---

9. WA 51, 191. See also LW 53, 388.

1947

I Want to Be a Farmer

THE FARM OF MY great-grandfather in Hettstedt filled me with excitement ever since my childhood. Dealing with the animals directly was surely one of the chief reasons. The living together of three generations; the regular daily routine; the simple but nourishing food; and being in the fresh air every day for a significant number of hours in "wind and weather" fascinated me. Between 1945 and 1949 I spent all of my free time and vacations on the farm in Hettstedt. I wanted to study agriculture and then direct a farm as a model farm, pursue new experiments in breeding animals and cultivating plants, and start a family with many children who feel comfortable on the land.

In 1948 I chose the theme "The Development of Agriculture in Germany during the Nineteenth Century" for my annual essay. In this connection I was also occupied with Damaschke's[1] thinking regarding land reform. What we experienced as land reform in the fall of 1945, namely, the dispossession of seven thousand large agricultural enterprises (400 morgen and larger) without compensation, had shocked and angered us particularly because of its inhumane implementation. In light of the numerous landless farmers from the East we considered a land reform to be entirely sensible. We did not consider it possible in 1947 that a few years later the dispossession of medium-sized farms and also a forced collectivization of small farms would follow. We still hoped for a reunification of Germany. The new

---

1. Adolf Wilhelm Ferdinand Damaschke (1865–1935) was a German politician and economist.

settlers who came in the fall of 1945 and had received 20 morgen of land to cultivate through the land reform set to work with great zeal. They built small adobe homes in which the barns and living quarters were under one roof, or they constructed homes and barns in the former estates. Some of the settlers did not succeed in this new beginning. Others expanded their area under cultivation by renting more land. About 3.3 million hectares of land were distributed as small parcels. The land reform in the fall of 1945 gave the farming industry in the eastern part of Germany a new perspective. Also, many children of farmers with mid-sized farms, like, for example, my woman cousin on my great-grandfather's farm, hoped in 1947 that there would be a revival of private farming. However, those were all illusions. The leadership of the Socialist Unity Party[2] had had the collectivization of farming in sight since 1945. As this was publicly announced in 1951 and 1952 and was also already attempted with the use of force, an emigration to West Germany from the villages began and grew constantly. The riots on June 16 and 17, 1953 stopped this development. Some collectivization by force was retracted, but only for a short time, as it soon turned out. The emigration then continued and increased. All independent farmers emigrated from some of the villages. However, the villages lost their identity even where they remained. Farms in the village were dissolved. Barns and stables were torn down or transformed into modern homes. The developing Agricultural Production Cooperatives became larger and larger entities and encompassed whole regions. The village communities no longer played a social role. That also affected the church communities in a devastating manner. Where the village church was located on a cemetery that was still used, it was relatively protected. It was used for worship services and funerals. However, the congregations became smaller and smaller and requested building permits for church buildings were granted less and less frequently. Consequently more and more church buildings were closed because of the building code.

In 1949 I chose the theme "The Isenheim Altar" by Matthias Grünewald[3] for my annual essay. My vocational wish had meanwhile changed. I wanted to become a pastor.

---

2. The Socialist Unity Party of Germany (Sozialistische Einheitspartei Deutschlands) was the Communist Party that eventually ruled the German Democratic Republic. The latter was officially dissolved on October 3, 1990 when the two Germanys were reunified.

3. Matthias Grünewald (c. 1480–1528), whose given name was Mathis Gothardt, was a painter of religious themes during the early sixteenth century. His most famous work is the altarpiece in the Antonine Monastery in Isenheim. He is particularly admired

1948

At the Stephaneum

I AM OBLIGED TO give particular thanks to two German teachers, Dr. Ottinger (1948–49) and Ms. von Oertzen (1949–50). Dr. Ottinger returned from the war with his health significantly impaired. In addition, his family was resettled from the East to Central Germany. Ms. von Oertzen experienced the same thing with her children. Her husband, an officer, was killed during the war.

In the first years after the war we had to manage without textbooks in the schools. This was a great challenge for the teachers but also an opportunity to design the instruction independently. During a time when the crimes of the National Socialists became more and more known and when we became aware of the whole extent of the destructions of the war, we occupied ourselves with Lessing[1] and the intellectual history of the Enlightenment. As we read and interpreted *Nathan the Wise* we searched for an answer to the question that afflicted all of us: "Why was something like the mass murder of the Jews in Germany possible?" The teacher sought

---

for the expressive nature of his art and his creative use of color and light in his paintings. It is not clear whether or not he supported the Reformation movement, although some Lutheran writings were among his possessions.

1. Gotthold Ephraim Lessing (1729–1781) was a writer, philosopher, and dramatist who was one of the chief representatives of the German *Aufklärung*, or Enlightenment, and made significant contributions both to philosophy and to German literature. While his own rationalistic perspectives caused him to reject the literal interpretation of Scripture and the notion of divine revelation, he was also an advocate of freedom of thought and of religious toleration. *Nathan the Wise* is generally considered to be his most influential work.

an answer together with us students. The ring parable of Nathan became the key experience for us. The truth can be found only with its acceptance. That applies to all spheres: religion, ideology, philosophy, and politics. We certainly felt how current the question still was. We Christians again had to remove the little confessional symbol "cross on the globe" when we entered our school. Whoever refused to congratulate the great Stalin on his birthday was suspected of being an enemy of socialism. We not only have to thank Dr. Ottinger for the discovery of the concept of toleration as the basic law for our way of life. He also allowed us to discover the beauty of the German language. We became enthused about Goethe's poems. We gladly learned the texts and competed in our presentations to the class. What a language! How miserable the use of German by the party was in comparison, both in the past and in the present.

Ms. von Oertzen made Goethe's *Faust* so contemporaneously relevant for us in the twelfth grade that the work became a source of life for us. We sensed in this woman how she searched for answers to her personal life questions in the poets and philosophers. Together with us she also discovered the new Bertolt Brecht, who was until then unknown to us. He had just returned from North America. He immediately won our hearts with his antiwar play *Mother Courage and her Children*.[2] His robust Luther German also thrilled us. Ms. von Oertzen smoothed the way to Brecht for me. I used many of his works in my parish ministry. The atheist Bertolt Brecht gave me many good ideas with his urgent, honest questions. Later I took advantage of every visit to Berlin in order to see a Brecht performance in the theater on the Schiffbauerdamm. Shortly before June 17, 1953[3] a staging of the original *Faust* by Brecht excited the emotions in Berlin. Brecht was severely attacked in *Neues Deutschland*[4] because his interpretation of Goethe's work harmed the party. After June 17 no one spoke further about this staging. For me the two great German poets and thinkers always be-

---

2. Hartmann shortens the title to *Mother Courage*.

3. After an initial uprising in East Berlin on June 16, 1953, large protests against the East German government occurred on the following day throughout the country, led particularly by workers who decided to strike and march in cities and towns. They protested especially against the social and economic implications of the continuing Sovietization of East Germany. The uprising was suppressed by the governmental authorities with the help of Soviet troops and armaments. See Chapter 1953.

4. *Neues Deutschland* was the official daily newspaper of the Socialist Unity Party in the German Democratic Republic and a chief means of propagating the party's perspectives.

longed closely together. I have to thank Ms. von Oertzen for this discovery. At that time, in the year 1950, in the twelfth grade, *Mother Courage and her Children* also strengthened our pacifistic stance. We could not believe that armed armies were again necessary in Germany four years after the war, and two armies, one in the East and one in the West at that. And they were supposed to point their weapons against each other, Germans against Germans. That was inconceivable to us!

1949

Two German States

WE FOLLOWED VERY ATTENTIVELY in our class how the construction of democracy was attempted in our society. The founding of the Socialist Unity Party of Germany through the union of the Communist Party of Germany and the Social Democratic Party of Germany on April 22, 1946 already made us suspicious. We were, nevertheless, surprised that the Socialist Unity Party of Germany could not achieve an absolute majority in the elections for the state parliament of Sachsen-Anhalt on October 20, 1946. The Christian Democratic Union (21.9 percent) and the Liberal Democratic Party of Germany (29.9 percent) had a combined strength that was greater than the Socialist Unity Party of Germany (45.8 percent) and the Peasants Mutual Aid Association (2.4 percent) combined. The Liberal Hübener[1] was elected as prime minister. However, because of pressure from the Soviets, the Christian Democratic Union and the Liberal Democratic Party of Germany were restricted more and more in their freedom. On December 19, 1947 the two chairpersons of the Christian Democratic Union in the

---

1. Erhard Hübener (1881–1958), who was one of the founders of the Liberal Democratic Party of Germany, was elected prime minister of Sachsen-Anhalt in 1946, although he was not a member of the Socialist Unity Party of Germany. He served until his resignation on October 1, 1949, shortly before the official founding of the German Democratic Republic. During his years of service he resisted reforms that the Soviet Union advocated and was a steadfast opponent of the division of Germany.

Two German States

East Zone, Jakob Kaiser[2] and Ernst Lemmer,[3] were removed from office by the Soviets. It appeared more and more that the occupying powers were pressing for two German states. The Bavarian government sought to prevent this by calling for an inter-zone conference in Munich on June 5, 1947. However, it was not even possible to agree on the agenda. The five prime ministers from the East left the conference on the same day when they noticed that their West German colleagues no longer wanted to nor could discuss a unified Germany. The western occupation powers had already settled on a West German state in the western defensive alliance while the Soviets still considered a neutral, united Germany. I can still remember that our geography teacher, who discussed political questions with us students quite candidly, blamed the western occupation powers and West German politicians indignantly and angrily the day after the failed Munich conference. We followed the further development attentively during the next months. The West Germans were always a step ahead of the East Germans on the way to two German states. The constitution of the Federal Republic of Germany was announced on May 23, 1949 and the constitution of the German Democratic Republic on May 30, 1949. From that year on there were two German states. At the time we considered it to be a temporary arrangement. None of us reckoned that this temporary arrangement would last forty years.

After the founding of the German Democratic Republic on October 7, 1949 the domestic policy sharpened within the GDR. We sensed this also in school. It was proposed that our school be renamed the Thomas Müntzer Secondary School. Thomas Müntzer[4] had been a teacher in our school for

2. Jakob Kaiser (1888–1961) was active as a labor union leader and opposed the Nazi government. After World War II he continued his labor union activity and was elected co-chairperson of the East German Christian Democratic Union. He was forced to resign this position by the Soviets in 1947, and he also had to leave East Berlin a year later. He joined the West German Christian Democratic Union, was elected its chairperson in 1950, and also served as a member of Konrad Adenauer's (1876–1967) cabinet from 1949 to 1957.

3. Ernst Lemmer (1898–1970) was both a news correspondent and a union leader before he was appointed co-chairperson of the East German Christian Democratic Union. Like his colleague Kaiser, he was removed from his office by the Soviets. He consequently moved to West Berlin and continued to be politically active. He served in several ministerial positions of the West German government, advocated for the reunification of Germany, and was a leader in fostering positive Jewish-Christian relationships.

4. Thomas Müntzer (1489–1525) was a sixteenth-century ecclesiastical and social reformer who became a leader of the peasants during the 1525 Peasants' War in the German territories. He was admired as a heroic revolutionary figure by the East German

some time. It was not officially discussed that he became a revolutionary as a theologian. Disastrous inferences for the present could, after all, have been drawn from this. Religion and Christianity could only be interpreted as dying movements. The fact that Gorky carried on a correspondence with Lenin regarding the societal role of religion had no significance for the party ideologues in the German Democratic Republic. It also became known soon that our director would be removed after our university qualification examination.[5] He would be replaced by a newly trained pedagogue who, of course, had to be a member of the Socialist Unity Party of Germany. The students were pressured more intensely to become members of the Free German Youth.[6] Those of us in the twelfth grade ascertained thankfully that we were able to enjoy the privilege of instruction free of ideology from 1945 until 1949.

---

governmental authorities.

5. The Abitur is a university qualifying examination that also marks a person's graduation from a secondary education institution, often referred to as Gymnasium, in the German context. A student passing the Abitur qualifies for further study at a university.

6. The Free German Youth (Freie Deutsche Jugend—FDJ) was the official, state-sponsored youth organization in the German Democratic Republic. All young people, aged fourteen to twenty-five, were expected to be members of this organization.

1950

A Night Hike

IN THE SUMMER OF 1950 I participated in a retreat for students preparing for the university qualifying examination that was sponsored by the church and took place in the Ilsenburg Abbey. A former military chaplain of a navy unit led the retreat. He was always properly dressed in pants with a sharp crease and a well-fitting jacket. During the devotions every word, every step, and every movement was given some thought.

Rector von Rhoden was completely different. He led in-depth Bible studies on texts from the Old Testament that sometimes transcended our ability to comprehend them. However, we sensed a spiritual and even prophetic passion in this man. It was said that he was in great demand as a chaplain[1] of pastors. The famous cantor Stier,[2] who very much shaped the singing movement in our churches, was also active in Ilsenburg at that time. His motto was "Singing keeps body and soul healthy." He was involved with the college for the continuing education of pastors and went into the countryside with older pastors in order to sing and practice breathing exercises. One of his students was engaged with those of us who were preparing for the examination. That was more of a joke for us at that time, but it was pleasant and relaxing.

---

1. Hartmann uses the term Seelsorger, which literally means "one who cares for the soul." The word is often used as a description of the pastoral office.

2. Alfred Stier (1880–1967) was both a composer and a church musician who served in the Evangelical Church of Saxony. In addition to composing chamber music, cantatas, choral works, and hymns, he was involved in the publication of extant sacred works. He was also active in promoting the work of church musicians and the use of music in the worship services of the church.

During the last night before our departure a group of us embarked on a nighttime hike on the Brocken.[3] We wanted to experience the sunrise on the summit. We set out around midnight, protected against the rain, and supplied with flashlights. We traveled on a steep hiking trail, always along the waterfalls of the Ilse River.

We arrived on the Brocken plateau precisely at 4 a.m. and were deeply disappointed. The summit of the Brocken was enveloped by fog, and it rained. We fled into the new train station, which had not yet been completed. Nevertheless, we had a roof over our heads. We gazed over an impenetrable sea of fog through a window opening that had not yet been glazed. Suddenly, there was a break in the fog for a short time, only for a few minutes. A wonderful, green landscape of woods and meadows into which were embedded villages and towns lay before us drenched in sunlight. Then dense patches of fog again blocked the view. However, the courage for the return hike was renewed. For a time we groped our way in the dense fog until the Bismarck rock. Suddenly the sun broke through, and the Harz spread out below us, far beyond the border between Germany and Germany.

We rested between stunted trees and tall huckleberry bushes and thought about our future. In a few hours our pathways parted. Some of us wanted to study theology, and others had totally different plans. Some were drawn to West Germany. Others intended to stay in the East. How would the two German states develop further?

We were eighteen years young. We still had our whole life before us. Filled with hope and curiosity we took our leave from one another.

---

3. The Brocken is the highest peak of the Harz, which is a mountain range that runs along the former border between East and West Germany.

1951

Campus Ministry in Halle

I WAS CLOSELY CONNECTED to the Evangelical campus ministry during the five years of my theological studies in Halle. Its chief event was the bible hour on Wednesday evening in the large hall of the city mission, which was attended by up to four hundred students. In addition, there were small circles in the individual faculties that addressed specific themes. In some faculties, for example, the medical and agricultural, there were a number of small circles. The pedagogical college, the Burg Giebichenstein,[1] and medical professional schools were also represented. I was engaged in the workgroup for foreign mission. An active choir assumed liturgical responsibilities during worship services (every two weeks because of an alternating pattern with the academic worship service). It also sang regularly in clinics and hospitals and even dared to perform oratorios. A circle of confidants, which was newly elected every semester, led the congregation, together with the campus pastor. During my first semester I attended a series of lectures on anthropological themes. Professors of all faculties participated, also natural scientists. Dr. Mende presented the last lecture and addressed the theme from a Marxist perspective. Because the auditorium could not accommodate all of the listeners, the lectures and discussions were transmitted through loudspeakers to other lecture halls and the stairway. The lecture series exceeded all expectations. A similar event was never again permitted at the university. However, as long as there were conscious

---

1. The Burg Giebichenstein is a college of art and design in Halle. Its present name is Burg Giebichenstein Hochschule für Kunst und Design Halle.

Christian professors on all the faculties, for example, the Professors Keller[2] (mathematics), Runge[3] (chemistry), Gallwitz[4] (natural sciences), and Hoffmann (agriculture), the campus ministry always gained new students every semester. A great sensation was aroused in the year 1953 when campus pastor Hamel was arrested and the members of the campus ministry were attacked in public gatherings, and at least some were threatened with expulsion. Courageous professors defended their students publicly at that time.

The Göttingen campus ministry was the partner congregation of the Halle community. There were a number of opportunities for engagement in Berlin and in Storkow, during the church conferences in Berlin or Leipzig, and during retreats in the Mansfeld Castle and elsewhere. I want to mention particularly the open evenings in the home of Pastor Hamel. The conversation played the crucial role at those times. In the campus ministry we experienced a democratic, that is, a collegial,[5] congregational leadership which we typically did not find in the church. There were also quite a few members of campus ministries who attempted to participate actively in the local congregations after their course of studies and who failed miserably because of the strong hierarchical structures of the congregations, yes, also of the Evangelical congregations. On the other hand, among the synodically active congregational members there were not a few who had gathered democratic experiences in a campus ministry. They could also introduce such experiences during the round tables after the Wende.[6] I also experienced prominent visitors through the campus ministry: for example, Pastor Martin Niemöller, who was in a concentration camp from 1937 to 1945 and who provoked a sensation because of the Stuttgart Declaration of

---

2. Ott-Heinrich Keller (1906–1990) was professor of mathematics at the Martin Luther University Wittenberg-Halle from 1951 until 1971.

3. Franz Rudolf Runge (1893–1973) taught chemistry at the university in Halle from 1947 until 1963.

4. Erich Walter Hans-Friedrich Gallwitz (1896–1958), generally known as Hans Gallwitz, taught geology and paleontology in Halle from 1946 until 1958 and served as Dean of the university from 1950 until 1952.

5. Hartmann uses the term geschwisterlich.

6. Wende literally means "change" or "turn." It has become the technical term used for the peaceful revolution that resulted in the fall of the Berlin Wall in 1989 and eventually of the East German government. The Wende ultimately led to the reunification of Germany in 1990. This reunification is also sometimes referred to as the Wende. Because of its significance and general use, the term is not translated.

Guilt[7] and because of his activities during the Easter marches.[8] Professor Hromádka[9] from Prague, the initiator of the Prague Peace Conference, was another visitor who impressed me greatly. Later, in the year 1968, he wrote a courageous letter to the Soviet ambassador after the Prague Spring.

---

7. On October 19, 1945 the Evangelical Church in Germany (Evangelische Kirche in Deutschland—EKD) declared publicly in the Stuttgart Declaration of Guilt that it had not sufficiently opposed the Nazi government and its policies. Martin Niemöller was a leading supporter of the declaration.

8. Peace marches, scheduled on the Monday after Easter, which is a traditional holiday in Germany, have occurred in Germany since 1960.

9. Josef Hromádka (1889–1969) was a Czech Protestant pastor, theologian, and professor who founded the Christian Peace Conference. He fled to the United States in 1939 because of the German occupation of Czechoslovakia and taught at Princeton Theological Seminary until 1946. He then returned to Prague where he resumed his professorship on the Comenius theological faculty. He was willing to cooperate with communist regimes because of his socialist convictions, but he opposed the discrimination against Christians by those regimes. He also protested the Soviet invasion of Czechoslovakia in 1968. He was an advocate of ecumenism and an active participant in the work of the World Council of Churches.

1952

My Conversions

AFTER MY CONFIRMATION IN the year 1946 I joined the Evangelical youth groups that were newly established throughout the country. Under the National Socialists only the youth work of the state was officially recognized after 1934. In 1946 the Mansfeld Castle, which was quite near to us, was offered to the church to be used as a retreat center for youth. Those of us from the surrounding villages often met there for weekend retreats, especially during the winter. We participated in fourteen-day retreats on specific themes. The state convention of the "Young Men Work"[1] met over the Pentecost holiday. About two hundred representatives of the youth groups from Sachsen-Anhalt gathered at the convention. I participated regularly starting in 1947. I had built up a youth group in my father's congregation in Burgörner, which I led until 1953. During these years I discovered under the influence of the youth counselors Fritz Hoffmann and Willi Reschke that Christian faith meant mandatory, consistent imitation of Christ. I joined the confessing company of singers:

> We march as the Youth Congregation[2] in defiance of the hardship of this time and call you, friends and foes, to join the sacred conflict.
>   We guard the fire for Christ the Lord in burning hearts. We light candles for the sake of love and show hope the star.

1. The Jungmännerwerk was a youth organization for young men of the Evangelical Church in the German Democratic Republic.

2. Junge Gemeinde was the term used for the youth group of an individual congregation of the Evangelical Church in the German Democratic Republic.

My Conversions

> We march, the Youth Congregation, and sense the step on our side. We do not fear devil or enemies for He, our Savior, accompanies us.

Under this influence many of us decided to study theology or to be trained as a deacon or church musician. During this time I discovered Dietrich Bonhoeffer's[3] book *The Cost of Discipleship* in my father's bookcase. I believed every word in the book of this martyr, who was executed in April 1945. This book, which was already published before the war, reinforced theologically what I had experienced in the Youth Congregation: everything depended on a mandatory imitation of Christ. I do not want to conceal that some of the youth counselors also warned us against a program of theological study. The course of studies could also destroy faith. I was particularly warned about the theologian Rudolph Bultmann[4] and his students. They would declare that many words of Jesus were later additions and describe letters of Paul as forgeries. Because I was warned about Bultmann, I occupied myself particularly intensively with him. While doing so I experienced my second conversion. Bultmann brought the whole New Testament to light as a book of proclamation. Words that Jesus delivered or texts of the four gospels interpreted and supplemented by disciples; special collections, like the passion story or healing stories; or collections of speeches, like the Sermon on the Mount, are all proclamation texts addressed to specific groups of people in a specific context. This is also applicable to the letters in precisely the same manner. In addition to the genuine letters of Paul there are letters by students of Paul who later on composed their congregational letters in the name of their master. The diverse addressees challenged the letter writers in special ways. There is a difference in whether one writes to

---

3. Dietrich Bonhoeffer (1906–1945) was a creative theologian and leader of the Confessing Church in Germany during the Nazi period. He was an early and persistent opponent of the persecution of the Jews and other policies of the National Socialists. As a result of his witness, he was imprisoned, sent to two concentration camps, and eventually executed. His *Cost of Discipleship* remains one of his most popular and influential writings.

4. Rudolf Bultmann (1884–1976) was a New Testament scholar who taught in Marburg from 1921 until 1951. He is known particularly for his focus on the proclamation of the New Testament rather than on the historical study of the biblical texts. He argued, therefore, that a focus on the New Testament *kerygma* of God's liberating work is more important than the quest for the historical Jesus. His notion of myth impacted biblical scholarship profoundly. During the Nazi period he was a member of the Confessing Church and a critic of the Nazi regime. However, he chose not to play an active role in opposing Nazi policies and ideology.

Jewish Christians or Gentile Christians, whether Romans or Greeks are the addressees, whether one appeals to the educated or to people with simple thought patterns. The New Testament thus contains sermons from the time between 30 and 100 CE that bear witness in a variety of ways that the Crucified One is the victor.

A book given to me as a gift in 1961, *Durchkreuzter Hass: Vom Abenteuer des Friedens*,[5] witnesses concretely what the victory means. That was my third conversion!

---

5. This volume, *Crossed-out Hatred: Concerning the Adventure of Peace*, was written by Rudolf Weckerling (1911–2014). There is apparently no English translation of the book. Weckerling was a German Lutheran pastor who joined the Confessing Church during the Nazi period and was imprisoned periodically during that time. His chief interests after the war were the promotion of peace, ecumenism, and Jewish-Christian dialogue. He served as a student pastor in Berlin and as a congregational pastor in Africa, the Middle East, and Berlin.

1953

June 17, 1953[1] in Halle

THE RUMORS FOLLOWED IN quick succession already early in the morning in Halle. Everyone brought her or his own variations about what presumably happened in Berlin the previous day. Work stoppage, strike, the employment of tanks against the demonstrators—that was unfathomable for us. I could not continue to participate in the theological seminar. What will be the response in Halle to the Berlin events? This question drove me into the street. I came to the marketplace.

Händel[2] on his monument, the towers of the Market Church, Roland on the Red Tower, the shops—they all had no ready answer. Even the town hall appeared as though it were closed. No one was visible on its broad steps.

I walked through the narrow Rathausgasse in the direction of the local court. As I came to the broad Hansering, I stopped as if I were frozen. A huge, colorful lindworm rolled along. It came from the Leipzig tower and was as wide as the street, including the sidewalks. As it came nearer it broke up into cheerful, enthusiastic groups of people. Some had flags and banners in their hands. Chatting, singing, in light summer clothing, they emitted a merry, hopeful mood. What a day!

1. See footnote 3 in chapter 1948.
2. Georg Friedrich Händel (1685–1759) was an influential Baroque composer who was born in Halle but moved to England in 1712. He was a gifted musician who produced both sacred and secular music, including oratorios, cantatas, organ concertos, anthems, and operas. The *Messiah,* one of his oratorios, remains a popular and well-known composition.

I could not remain standing on the sideline. The colorful lindworm swallowed me up. I learned that they were all from Ammendorf, particularly from the railcar factory. They intended to occupy the capital of the district and to support here the demands of the Berlin construction workers from the Stalinallee. I learned as we proceeded that the workers of the Leunawerke[3] were on their way to Merseburg. There were supposedly work stoppages throughout the German Democratic Republic on this day.

There was a great traffic jam near the main post office in the Grossen Steinstrasse. Another colorful lindworm was also pressing its way into the Grossen Steinstrasse from the Marx-Engelsplatz. Where the two lindworms dissolved into each other two huge signs were torn down from the front of the post office building with thundering applause and trampled by hundreds of feet. The almighty chairman of the German Democratic Republic's council of state, Walter Ulbricht,[4] was pictured on one of the signs. The demonstrators cheered: "The Goatee[5] must be removed." I no longer remember who was pictured on the other sign. Definitely not Stalin! His picture would not have been torn down, for during the morning we all still hoped that Russian troops would refrain from acting.

Some display windowpanes were also broken during the laborious progression in the direction of the market square. However, people were careful not to loot. The demonstrators wanted to present their just demands in a disciplined and orderly manner, and they hoped that the governmental authorities would be willing to hold talks. In this way we encouraged each other in our early summer mood. As our protest march rolled onto the market square, we were welcomed by indescribable jubilation. Where a gaping void ruled two hours earlier, thousands of women, men, and youth were now pressing into the market square. And the crowd continued to grow. All of the streets that led to the market square continually spat new demonstrators into the bustling crowd gathered there.

The strike leadership informed the demonstrators regarding the most current situation over loudspeakers. Delegates from the Mansfeld region,

3. This was the largest chemical factory in the German Democratic Republic, located in Leuna, south of Halle.

4. Walter Ulbricht (1893–1973) was one of the founders of the Communist Party of Germany during the Weimar Republic. He lived in exile in France and Russia during the Nazi period. After returning to Germany, he played a crucial role in the establishment of the German Democratic Republic and served as head of state from 1960 until 1973, during which time he cooperated closely with the Soviet government.

5. Walter Ulbricht wore a goatee. The demonstrators were voicing a bold call for the removal of the leader of the government.

from the Leunawerke, and from Bitterfeld expressed their solidarity with us. We received some information about the events in Berlin. We were repeatedly urged to remain calm and disciplined. In Halle the municipal council had agreed to meetings with the strike leadership. The provisioning of the city was guaranteed. There was no need for panic buying.

An armored vehicle, which appeared suddenly, caused a stir. It stopped before the entrance to the Little Market Castle.[6] A man was invited into the vehicle and brought to the city hall. An official probably no longer felt safe. The demonstrators reacted with derision and ridicule.

Thirty minutes later a pistol shot whipped over our heads nearby. Excited screams followed. A throng of people surged through the crowd in the direction of the Eselsmarkt. "Grab him. He is the one who shot!" Apparently, an official was recognized and reacted in panic by shooting into the air.

New rumors spread through the crowd unceasingly. The remand prison on the Hansering was presumably stormed. All persons in custody were supposedly freed. Were violent criminals also among them? There were supposedly also shots at the Roten Ochsen.[7] Presumably some people were killed. An attempt to free prisoners there apparently failed.

It worried us gradually that there were repeated warnings about provocations against Soviet troops. Was the strike leadership already in doubt regarding the restraint of the Soviet troops? Had it perhaps already received troubling news from other cities? The rumor eventually went around that at 6 p.m. a mass rally was going to happen on the Hallmarkt[8] with prominent representatives of strike organizations from the industrial regions of Leuna, Buna, Ammendorf, the Mansfeld territory, Bitterfeld, and Wolfen. Speakers from Berlin were also expected. We moved from the market square to the Hallmarkt with much jostling and shoving, but in a disciplined manner. The rebels met today where the ruling party had usually carried out their prescribed mass gatherings.

The demands of the strikers to the government were repeated again and again: reduction of the labor standards, higher wages, abolition of the

6. The Marktschlösschen is not a castle but a sixteenth-century, Renaissance-style building on the market square in Halle. The origin of its name is not certain, but its appearance may be the reason for the name. There was also a restaurant by that name in the building over a century ago. The Marktschlösschen is now owned by the city of Halle and has been used for exhibits and commercial purposes.

7. The Rote Ochsen was a penitentiary in Halle. The reason for its name is uncertain, although it may be related to the color of its walls. It now serves as a memorial.

8. The Hallmarkt is a western section of downtown Halle.

agricultural and craft cooperatives that were enforced by law, closing of the state-owned stores, freedom of speech and of the press, and an independent justice system. The demands were enthusiastically approved. Suddenly some jarring cries were heard among the multitude: "Revenge for injustice! Hang the officials! Kill the communist pigs!" The gathering whistled these demands down and agreed with the strike leadership, which distanced itself angrily from these outbursts of hate. During the following days we learned that a small group of freed prisoners with a Nazi past had made such hateful demands. The key figure in this group was Ms. Erna Dorn,[9] who supposedly played a wicked role as supervisor of the Ravensbrück concentration camp. She was condemned to death a few days after June 17 and executed in October, without a proper process, as I now know.

The massive crowd of people remained with an increasing inner tension. What will we hear? What is the situation in Berlin now? Suddenly a single trumpet sounds high above our heads. A single trumpeter stands on the bridge between the Hausmann towers.[10] He plays several choral melodies. When a trumpet ensemble plays twice a week from the Hausmann towers, their music is often lost in the traffic noise. On June 17 many agitated people listened to the soft voice of a single trumpet. It awakened hope, on which we were urgently dependent.

Because not much later terrible noises, which came nearer and nearer and became more and more threatening, frightened us. Soviet tanks appeared and turned into the Hallmarkt. Their gun barrels were pointed at the speaker platform. Urgent pleas came from the platform: do not let them provoke you! Perhaps the tanks are coming with friendly intentions?

The crowd gave way to the approaching tanks, let them pass through, and merged together again behind them. There were eventually eight or ten tanks that stood on the Hallmarkt, incorporated into the collection of people that numbered 100,000. The ever-increasing noise made by motors

---

9. Erna Dorn (1911–1953) remains a controversial figure since her activities are interpreted in various ways. She was definitely an ardent supporter of the Nazi regime and worked in Ravensbrück, the largest concentration camp for women. Her precise role there is unclear, but she was condemned as a war criminal by the authorities of the German Democratic Republic in 1951 and sentenced to fifteen years in prison. She was freed from prison during the June 17, 1953 uprising but was recaptured when she participated in the events that Hartmann described and was found guilty of treason. Her precise motivation for her activity on June 17 remains unclear and the justification for her condemnation and execution continues to be debated. There is little doubt about her sympathies for the Nazi regime, however.

10. The two towers of the Market Church in Halle are named the Hausmann towers.

and chains from the surrounding streets made it unmistakably clear that the whole city was currently being occupied by Soviet troops. Was everything already lost now?

A desperate member of the strike committee, dressed in a police or a soldier's uniform, climbs onto the wall cornice of the platform, extends his arms, and calls to the tanks: "Freedom!" Another appeals to the demonstrators to go home now quietly. A curfew has been established for the evening. However, tomorrow we intend to congregate here again at the same time. Everything is not yet lost!

During the dissolution of the huge gathering a small protest march, which wanted to pass through the city center, still organized itself. The German flag, without the emblem of the German Democratic Republic, was carried ahead of it. Someone carrying a picture of Thälmann walked behind it. Two songs were sung alternately, the third verse of the German national anthem and the song of the laborers, "Brothers, to the sun, to freedom..." I walked with the group for a distance. The group of demonstrators became constantly smaller. We saw that the orders of the Soviet commanding officer of the city were glued to the walls of the houses everywhere. One could read plainly: "Whoever opposes the orders will be shot."

I had to hurry so that I could reach my student apartment on the south side of the city before curfew.

1954

Hamburg, Gateway to the World[1]

ONE OF MY MOTHER'S cousins had invited me to visit in Hamburg. That was still possible in 1954. I began my journey with great expectations. I did not know any of the Hamburg relatives. They also did not know me, but they had a photograph of me when I was a child. How would we recognize each other in the large main train station? I already heard about major strikes in Hamburg on the train. The city was dark, and none of the streetcars would be operating since the power station workers were striking for higher wages. I waited on the train platform until almost all the travelers had left it. Then I looked around and saw a happy couple on a bench. They held a small photo and compared every male traveler with the picture. It was immediately clear to me that they could only be my relatives. I went toward them and introduced myself. In this way I met my Uncle Helmut who maintained an honest political dialogue with me during the coming decades, in spite of the construction of the wall, travel limitations, and surveillance of the mail. Unfortunately, he did not live to see the fall of the Berlin wall.

I conquered Hamburg, the proud Hanseatic city, in fourteen days. All the rubble from the horrible nights of bombing had already been cleared. The architects prepared the plans for rebuilding. I initially stayed close to the airport, and I spent some time there daily. Airplanes from all over the world landed there continuously. Passengers from all continents exited the machines. How confined we lived in the German Democratic Republic. I was overcome by a painful desire for faraway places!

1. The Hamburg port is known as Germany's "Gateway to the World."

During the second week I stayed in the city center and only had to travel a few stations to reach the wharf. The previous day I informed myself by means of the daily newspaper about which ships, from which countries, would dock at which pier. The next morning I was on site and marveled and was excited. I reached the grounds of the port by means of the Elbe Tunnel, which survived the bombing attacks in good condition.

One day a harbor worker spoke to me on the port grounds. He had discovered the little confessional symbol "cross on the globe" on my jacket. How can a young human being still believe in God after the horrible war, after Auschwitz, and after Hiroshima? That was his question. He quickly brought up the church, which, after all, has failed so often. I did not contradict him and let him know that those are also my own questions. Then I told him that I come from the German Democratic Republic, how I experienced June 17 in the previous year, and how despairing and disappointed many of our people are, particularly also those who had bravely resisted during the Nazi period. The harbor worker listened carefully and beckoned one of his coworkers who was just passing by. He stopped and joined the conversation. They both admitted that they had not yet considered the whole problem from the perspective of the people in the German Democratic Republic. I stated that it is everywhere and always crucial that there are people who do not abandon their hope. Some draw their hope from faith in Jesus of Nazareth. Others draw it from music or nature or from a philosophical system or from the program of a political party. What is important is that we all respect each other. It depends on everyone who has hope!

Thirty years later, as Christians and non-Christians in the German Democratic Republic found themselves together in civil rights groups in order to make our country a bit more humane, we encouraged one another with the motto: "A hope learns to walk."

1955

Vicar in Lindau

AFTER MY FIRST THEOLOGICAL examination I was called to a vicarage on November 1, 1955. Initially I lived four weeks with my vicarage supervisor, the Superintendent Henke, in Droysig near Zeitz. At the end of November I moved to the parsonage in Lindau near Eisenberg. I was welcomed in a friendly manner in the little rural village. Two church elders guided me through the village, along the single road in the village, and explained to me which farm family lived on which farm. They had also organized by which farmers who had already retired I could be provided for at noon meals. At the conclusion of the tour they showed me the church. They stopped at two graves in the cemetery in which the last two pastors were buried. It seemed to me as if the farmers wanted to say: "Perhaps you will also like being among us so well that you will remain in the village until your death." I was twenty-three years old at that time! By no means did I want to consider such circumstances!

    The pastor's widow, who had moved just a few days before my arrival, had nicely furnished some modest rooms for me in the parsonage. Two older ladies, sisters who came from Tilsit, also lived in the parsonage. They considered me to be a protector. They would now no longer have to fear wicked burglars. When I was not at home they received the mail and gave it to me sorted in two parts, official and private. They must have always studied the sender very carefully. One morning when I was just having breakfast the woman mail carrier brought a small package. I placed it next to the cheese with the intention of opening it after breakfast. However, I wanted to ascertain the sender immediately. I read "crematorium." I was horrified. It was the urn with the remains of a nice man who had died a few days earlier from cancer. I ran through the apartment all flustered holding the urn package and looked for a dignified place for the urn. Then it occurred to me that such a place could only be in the church. I carried the urn into the church and placed it on a small table in the chancel.

A few days earlier I was informed from the neighboring Rudelsdorf, which belonged to the parish of Lindau, that a young girl died in Jena during a brain operation. The mother in Rudelsdorf received this information two hours previously. She was all alone in her sorrow since she was a widow and her other children lived far away. I should go visit her at once. I left immediately but was completely helpless. What should I say to the poor mother? What will she expect from a pastor? I found her crying in the kitchen. I introduced myself and sat down quietly beside her. She told me about her daughter, about her childhood and her vocational plans. She showed me pictures of her daughter. Because she was so beautiful she had already had several admirers. Suddenly the mother spoke of her faith in God who would give her strength and support. She knows of no answer to the question: "Why must a seventeen-year-old young woman die during a brain operation?" I also had no answer. I sat quietly the whole time. The mother talked and cried the whole time. Suddenly she jumped up and thanked me that I had visited her. The neighbors are all of no help! I stammered a few sentences about my helplessness and left. A neighboring pastor would lead the memorial service.

This is how I experienced my vicarage, closely integrated into an intimate village community, in ecclesiastical catechesis, in building and rental matters, in church anniversary celebrations . . .

1956

Seminary in Brandenburg

I LOOKED FORWARD TO the community at the seminary after my first practical ministry attempts during the vicarage. I was called to Brandenburg and met young theologians there from the Brandenburg, Pomeranian, Silesian, and Province Saxony territorial churches. All brought their positive and less positive experiences from vicarage with them. Our supervisor, Jürgen Henkys,[1] was only a few years older than we were and showed great understanding when our frustrations burdened us significantly at times. Our director, Albrecht Schönherr,[2] was highly respected by all of us as a student of Bonhoeffer and as a representative of an ecclesiastical opposition in the territory of Bishop Otto Dibelius who had just negotiated a military chaplaincy agreement with Chancellor Adenauer. However, we credited our

---

1. Jürgen Henkys (1929–2015) made a significant contribution to the musical heritage of the church in Germany by translating a variety of hymns into German, particularly from the Dutch, English, and Norwegian languages. He also taught practical theology at the Humboldt University in Berlin.

2. Albrecht Schönherr (1911–2009) was a Lutheran pastor who served the church in the German Democratic Republic in various capacities, including as superintendent of Brandenburg on the Havel, director of the seminary in Brandenburg on the Havel, general superintendent of the Eberswalde diocese, bishop of the eastern region of the Evangelical Church in Berlin-Brandenburg, and chairperson of the Association of Evangelical Churches in the German Democratic Republic. He promoted the notion of "church in Socialism" with the intention of gaining substantial autonomy for the church by agreeing to avoid direct confrontation with the state. Such an agreement was reached on March 6, 1978 between Schönherr and the political leader of the German Democratic Republic, Erich Honecker (1912–1994).

director particularly because he wanted to keep in contact with us when we had to prove ourselves independently in our first congregations. It was a great concern for him to integrate us into a far-reaching spiritual community. He saw with great concern how many pastors struggle on the front line in isolation and quickly capitulate. He discussed with us Bonhoeffer's vision of a communio sanctorum[3] and the work of the brothers of Taizé.

A thorough exegesis always preceded the practical catechetical and homiletical work. I learned more about Old Testament and New Testament theology in Brandenburg than during my theological studies in Halle. I only truly comprehended in Brandenburg what the meaning of Bonhoeffer's "church for others"[4] was. South American liberation theology, the activities of the French worker priests, the worldwide spiritual community of the Brothers of Taizé, but also the efforts of Horst Symanowski[5] to establish an ecclesiastical presence in the industrial working world (see his seminars in Mainz-Kastell!) all belonged together and moved us greatly in Brandenburg. I came to recognize that I wanted to work in industry for a time before I became involved in parish work.

In the spring, our seminary was invited by the North German churches. Officially we could not travel to West Germany as a seminary. Each one of us requested permission to travel individually and then met by chance on the train. The German Democratic Republic officials did not notice, or acted as though they did not notice. To our great surprise, the officials in the West reacted quite differently. They speculated that we were a Free German Youth group who wanted to do a propaganda tour in the Federal Republic of Germany. When we became tired of the questioning and the interrogations (we all had to leave the train!), we acknowledged that we were traveling as a group from the seminary in Brandenburg because of an invitation from the North German churches. The police officials reacted greatly irritated and almost offended. As the train entered the Hamburg main train station, the Brandenburg seminary was cordially greeted by means of the

---

3. Bonhoeffer published an ecclesiastical study with the title Sanctorum Communio in 1930.

4. Bonhoeffer, *Letters and Papers*, 382.

5. Horst Symanowski (1911–2009) was an Evangelical pastor who joined the Confessing Church, opposed Hitler, sought to protect Jewish families, and was imprisoned several times. After the war he became particularly interested in serving and promoting the rights of workers. He was also a peace advocate, opposed nuclear armaments, and served on the editorial board of the progressive ecclesiastical journal, *Die Stimme der Gemeinde*.

loudspeaker. The next morning there were reports in all the newspapers. This was done with positive intentions but, at the same time, it also became clear how little we knew about each other. Our seminary director must have experienced many problems when he returned to Brandenburg. During our trip we were guests in Hamburg, Oldenburg, and Bremen. The meeting with young theologians in training at the seminary in Preetz in Schleswig-Holstein was particularly valuable for me. Naturally, the agreement regarding military chaplaincy was also an important topic here.

1957

The Black Pump

INSPIRED BY HORST SYMANOWSKI's industrial seminars in Mainz-Kastell and by the example of the French worker priests, I decided to interrupt my normal course of training and work in an industry for a time. Bishop Jänicke[1] in Magdeburg encouraged me in my views and granted me the requisite leave. I initially sought employment in the Mansfeld copper mining industry but did not succeed. However, I then found the possibility of work in the brown coal collective called Black Pump, which was at that time the largest industrial complex in the German Democratic Republic.

I worked as miner in the state-run industry Talsperrenbau Weimar for eight months (September 1, 1957 to April 30, 1958). Our factory built the drainage systems for the developing brown coal collective Black Pump. I wrote an extensive report about my experiences, which I presented to the Magdeburg church leadership in the summer of 1958. I discovered a copy of the report in 1991 in my Halle State Security Service file among other papers in my ecclesiastical personal file. An informant of the State Security Service must have copied it in the consistory.

The report makes it clear that I considered my industrial work as ecclesiastical service from the very beginning. Like Bonhoeffer, I was convinced

---

1. Johannes Jänicke (1900–1979) served as bishop of the Evangelical Church of the Church Province Saxony from 1955 until 1968. He was an active member of the Confessing Church during the Nazi period and thereafter an important leader of the Evangelical church in the German Democratic Republic. He was particularly involved in the peace movement and promoted the option of alternative service for conscientious objectors. His wife, Eva Rudolphi Jänicke (1901–1965) was an eager supporter of and, at times, participant in the ministry of Jänicke.

that the church did not have the authority to speak at that moment. Our assignment consists now of "praying and doing justice among the people." As we do, we must confidently wait for the day "when human beings are again called to proclaim the word of God in such a way that the world is changed and renewed thereby."[2] In my case, I understood "doing justice" as nothing more than placing myself on an equal footing with the miners, sharing their work with them, and living with them.

I organized the report of my experience into four parts: the factory; life in the camp; the worldview of the worker; and implications for the work of the church. I will attempt to summarize my 1958 report briefly.

THE FACTORY

Black Pump was a large industrial complex in which many specialized firms worked side by side. As such, it was an exceptional manufacturing situation. Specialists and laborers worked here. They came from all parts of the German Democratic Republic and some also from the Federal Republic of Germany. Brigade and site foremen played an important role. It depended on them whether one earned much or little. Their "sharp pencil" decided. I worked in a "muck brigade" which only provided unskilled labor. It was difficult physical labor on the cement mixer; when transporting cement, rails, and water pipes; when draining ditches; and when extracting pine tree roots, and so on. And we did all of this during any kind of weather, including when it rained or in twenty-degree cold. As we did this kind of work, we recognized how dependent we were on one another. For example, when ten workers picked up a railroad rail in order to move it, no one could trip or fail to carry the load. That could have meant serious injuries for his colleagues. My colleagues were not inclined to speak positively about the office workers in their warm barrack rooms. I could understand them very well when we had to work outside in the snow and the cold. It was pure envy. The laborers imagined that the office workers drank coffee most of the time and occasionally also wrote something. I found my work colleagues to be good and helpful companions. I did not become one of them. I was, after all, only among them as a visitor. They were glad about this visit. However, I could return to my world again at any time. They had to remain here as the

---

2. Bonhoeffer, *Letters and Papers*, 380.

"condemned of this earth."³ They also had no hope for a political change four years after June 17, 1953.

LIFE IN THE CAMP

I lived in a village twenty kilometers away during the first three months. I traveled from there to the collective every day in a factory bus. The difference between the traditional Sorbendorf (with traditional costumes for festive days and for daily use and an overcrowded church every Sunday!) and the large industrial site, which wholly transformed an old cultural landscape, could not have been greater. After three months, I found lodging in the residential camp of the factory. Five colleagues were housed in one barrack room. In addition to the barracks used for lodging, there were also a commercial kitchen, the pub Die Schwemme, the cultural barrack with a library, the outpatient clinic, a grocery, a barbershop, a shoe repair shop, a tailor shop, and a laundry in the camp, which was located ten kilometers from Hoyerswerda in the middle of a wooded area. The available cultural events were very minimally attended. Political propaganda events with anti-Christian themes, such as "Sputnik and God" or "Scientific worldview and religious superstition," only attracted a few listeners when they were accompanied by free movies. I was able to have good conversations, particularly about the works of Bertolt Brecht, which I studied with great enthusiasm at that time, with the head of the library and with a young party member who had to complete a practicum at a large industrial site after attending the training institution of the party.

A Roman Catholic church was located near the residential camp in which both Roman Catholic and Evangelical worship services took place. I met worshippers from the residential camp only seldom. In the camp it was primarily members of free churches and of sects who professed to be Christians. During my free time I gathered a group of people, Christians and non-Christians, who were interested in religious matters. Our group quickly attracted the attention of the State Security Service. The informer who was assigned to us, a West German, soon admitted this to me.

---

3. Hartmann does not indicate that this is the case, but he is likely quoting the title of a book by Franz Fanon (1925–1961). *Les Damnés de la Terre* was published in 1961, with a foreword by Jean-Paul Sartre (1905–1980). The English translation of the work is titled *The Wretched of the Earth*. In this volume Fanon, who has significantly influenced postcolonial perspectives and scholarship, analyzes the destructive impact of colonialism on individuals and nations.

THE WORLDVIEW OF THE WORKER

The workers have a very distinct class consciousness. They are cohesive, practice solidarity with each other, but feel betrayed by their representatives in the labor union and party. They believe in technological progress that will ease the daily labor of the proletariat more and more. They are enthused about every new industrial machine, and the first Sputnik in space could truly fascinate them.

Their fear of wars and their desire for peace are convincing. However, they have an unerring sense regarding hypocrisy and propaganda. They deny the Socialist Unity Party of Germany the right to describe itself as progressive and peace-loving. I was surprised by the self-righteousness of my fellow workers over against prisoners from Cottbus and Bautzen who had to work near us. "They must have some kind of dirt under their carpets."[4] This was the general opinion. I attempted to enable them to understand the prisoners better as unfortunate people and pointed out that criminals and political prisoners were mixed together in the brigades. I found no one willing to listen.

Women were, of course, the chief topic of their conversations. Innumerable incredible stories about women were told with boundless exaggerations. The second main topic was sport. Faith in God belonged to the topics that were not discussed. It is remarkable that they liked the celebrative elements of church. We young theologians wanted plain worship services, without liturgy, in simple church halls that were to resemble factory interiors. However, those who were estranged from the church, whom we wanted to reach in this way, looked particularly for the special in the church, not the ordinary. Baroque churches, many candles, much gold, the pastor in the clerical robe, festive organ music. This is what the tough workers wanted to experience when they did go to church once in a while.

IMPLICATIONS FOR THE WORK OF THE CHURCH

The pastor is always viewed in a very reserved manner by the workers. He is already a stranger to them because he is an educated person. Socially the pastor belongs to another class. A pastor who intentionally behaves in a friendly and jovial manner is viewed very warily. A pastor who is "real"

---

4. The German colloquial saying, "Sie werden schon irgendwelchen Dreck am Stecken haben," means "They must be guilty of something."

is convincing. Even if the pastor is somewhat eccentric, what is essential is that he speaks and lives credibly.

Luther demands at the beginning of his Romans lectures that the pastor must differentiate between his office and himself, between the "form of God" and the "form of the servant."[5] The people who live "below"[6] understand this differentiation better than we might think!

This is the summary of my 1958 report.

I made contact with Bruno Schottstädt[7] from the Gossner Mission in Berlin during my time of working in the Black Pump. I experienced a great deal of helplessness in my queries in Spremberg (Brandenburg Church) and in Hoyerswerda (Silesian Church). The church was not prepared for the Black Pump collective. In the following year General Superintendent Jacob[8] of Cottbus together with the Gossner Mission organized ecclesiastical missions in the Black Pump, in Lübbenau, and in Cottbus.

---

5. WA 56, 161. See also LW 25, 140.

6. Bonhoeffer speaks of viewing the events of history "from below" in his *Letters and Papers*, 17. Hartmann's perspectives were obviously impacted by the insights of Bonhoeffer.

7. Bruno Schottstädt (1927-2000) was an Evangelical pastor who founded the Gossner Mission in 1954, even before his ordination. The Gossner Mission sought to witness the gospel through the practical service of human beings in their work environments. Schottstädt was also interested in ecumenical and missionary work and supported the peace movement in the German Democratic Republic.

8. Günter Jacob (1906-1993) was one of the founders of Pastors' Emergency League and a member of the Confessing Church during the Nazi rule. He was arrested a number of times and forbidden to speak about political matters publicly. Having been drafted in 1939, he fought on the Eastern front. After the war, he resumed his pastoral ministry and served as general superintendent in Lübben and in Cottbus. From 1963 until 1967 he also functioned as part-time administrator of the bishop's office of the eastern region of the Evangelical Church Berlin-Brandenburg. He published a number of books and was given an honorary doctorate by the University of Tübingen.

1958

First Pastorate, Mücheln

AT THE END OF February, after work, I found an official letter from the bishop of Magdeburg among the plates, cups, and newspapers that had not yet been cleared from the table in our barrack room. Many fingerprints proved that many curious people must have held it in their hands with astonishment. What might be the explanation for the presence of a bishop's letter in the Black Pump? I suspected it. Bishop Dr. Jänicke inquired whether I was ready to accept a pastorate in the industrial congregation Mücheln near Merseburg. After several days of reflection I accepted the invitation. In the summer I transitioned from the collective Black Pump to the pastorate of the St. James congregation in Mücheln in the brown coal region of the Geisel River valley.

As I registered in the town hall, there was much confusion when I indicated on the questionnaire that I most recently worked as a miner. There was a spontaneous conversation about church and the world of labor. I could not have wished for a better start. I could make it clear that the church cannot allow itself to be pushed back into a kind of ghetto. We understand ourselves as "church in the society." Our city is divided into three parts: the old city; a housing development with single-family homes in gardens from the time of the Weimar Republic; and a housing development of log houses built after 1945 and populated, in part, by families from the razed villages.

My chief foci in my work during the first years were the confirmation program, youth ministry, visits in the newly built section of the town, the ecumenical week of prayer, Bible and catechism weeks, fostering

First Pastorate, Mücheln

participation of lay members in the worship services and the congregational evening meetings, and the organization of a regional academic circle. I found the resignation of my older colleagues after the defeat in the struggle against the youth consecration[1] to be disheartening. Parents and youth placed their hope in me that the church would remain welcoming, also to participants in the youth consecration. I was fortunate that four other theologians similar to me in age had begun their service in our church district at the same time that I did. We met separately, in addition to the official ecclesiastical meetings, and worked theologically and strategically on the themes that can be summarized under the general topic "church in society."

The population was kept in a state of unrest because of persistent new occurrences. Private businesses were transformed into commercial cooperatives or supermarket cooperatives overnight. Artisans were forced to join production cooperatives. Farmers sought to retain some independence in Type III[2] rural cooperatives. There were also many people in Mücheln who had no more hope and emigrated to West Germany.

In a word from the pulpit addressed to the congregations, our bishop asked the members of the congregations to remain in the German Democratic Republic, in spite of the difficulties. On Saturday before the presentation of the bishop's message, we pastors were visited by representatives of the state and warned not to read the bishop's letter. He would exceedingly exaggerate the problem. Of course, we read the letter but, to our surprise, we experienced that members of the congregations reacted angrily, especially those who had some relatives who had already left for West Germany. When the neighboring pastor of the St. Ulrich congregation in Mücheln also did not return from a vacation trip to West Germany, the consternation

---

1. The Jugendweihe, or youth consecration, was a political, state-sponsored alternative to confirmation in the German Democratic Republic. The study of the Marxist-Leninist worldview, rather than of Scripture and Christian theology, was the focus of instruction. Residents of the German Democratic Republic who refused to participate in the Jugendweihe because of their Christian convictions were given fewer educational and economic opportunities. There were debates within the church whether participants in the Jugendweihe would still be welcomed as members of the church. During the 1950s, participation in the Jugendweihe was strongly opposed by the church. Because the vast majority of young people participated, however, the church ultimately adopted a pragmatic perspective, particularly in light of the operative vision "church in society."

2. Type III rural cooperatives required the farmers to relinquish all property related to farming to the cooperative, while Type I and Type II cooperatives still allowed farmers to retain some land, livestock, and other property. Type III cooperatives were the ultimate goal of the communist system in East Germany.

was oppressive. Hamel's[3] little book *Christ in der DDR*[4] was a great help to us during that time. We began a learning process here in the East, namely, that in a society ruled dictatorially by an atheistic political party we have to bear witness to the incarnate God. Therefore, it makes sense to remain here!

---

3. Johannes Hamel (1911–2002) was an Evangelical theologian and teacher. He was a member of the Confessing Church, opposed Nazi policies, and assisted Jewish Christians. As a result, he was forced to work in the Leuna works, the largest chemical factory in Germany, and was also drafted. He was wounded as a soldier and became a prisoner of war in Italy. After the war he was campus pastor in Halle and defended the youth ministry of the church against the governmental authorities who opposed it. As a result, he was imprisoned, though ultimately freed because of international protests. During his imprisonment he became convinced that even his opponents deserved to be treated as fellow human beings and were to be offered the gospel and forgiveness. He also decided to remain in the German Democratic Republic. From 1955 until 1976 he taught practical theology in the Katechetisches Oberseminar in Naumburg (Saale), where students could study theology with instructors who were not directly under the authority of the state. He also served as rector of this institution periodically.

4. Hamel, *Christ in der DDR*. See also Hamel, *A Christian in East Germany*.

1959

Bliss with Tent and Bicycle

WE WERE MARRIED BY my father in the St. Maurice Church in Naumburg on August 12. Children with a rope blocked our way during our festive exit from the church. They asked for a ransom. Fortunately, I had made provision. I threw pennies, five-penny coins, and ten-penny coins[1] among the children. They scuffled over each coin. However, we now had an open path. We walked with our guests along the Saale to the seafood restaurant of the Schulpforta Cloister. The hosts, who were old acquaintances of the Kühn family, had prepared a festive table for us there out in the open.

The next day we set out on our honeymoon trip to Mecklenburg as a newly married couple, equipped with bicycles and a very tiny tent made in Poland. We traveled by train to Neustrelitz, climbed on the bicycles, and reached a very beautiful meadow on the Schwarzer See, having traveled through Mirow.

We had everything all to ourselves: the lake, the meadow, the forest on a peninsula in the lake, the fresh air, the sun, and the singing of the birds. From time to time, we experienced a cow sticking her head into the tent inquisitively very early in the morning and mooing us a morning greeting. Sometimes the old village pastor from Schwarz brought us fresh fruit and vegetables from his garden. When he came near our tent, he cleared his throat considerately and waited until one of us stuck our head out of the tent.

We experienced lovely weeks in the most cramped space, in the smallest tent, in the vast Mecklenburg region. A new time had begun for us

1. Groschen

young lovers. The sensitive poet states what we felt for each other in this way in the Song of Solomon:

> I am a rose of Sharon, a lily of the valleys.
>
> As a lily among the brambles, so is my love among maidens.
>
> As an apple tree among the trees of the wood, so is my beloved among young men.
>
> With great delight I sat in his shadow, and his fruit was sweet to my taste.
>
> He brought me to the banqueting house, and his intention toward me was love.
>
> Sustain me with raisins, refresh me with apples; for I am faint with love.
>
> O that his left hand were under my head, and that his right hand embraced me!
>
> I adjure you, O daughters of Jerusalem, by the gazelles or the wild does; do not stir up or awaken love until it is ready! (Song 2:1–7 NRSV)

Happy and curious, we traveled to Mücheln near Merseburg, into the heart of the brown coal region, in the middle of September. A small parsonage waited for us there, the three-hundred-year-old diaconate. It became our first home together.

1960

Summer along the Volga

DURING AN AUGUST WEEKEND things worked out. Thanks be to God! Our travel documents were handed to us at the Soviet embassy Unter den Linden. A three-week period of struggling with the German and the Russian authorities had led to a positive conclusion.

At 4 a.m. the train from the Berlin-East train station to Moscow was on its way. We shared the compartment with two young women teachers. This was their first trip to Russia, as it was for us. A friendly Russian railroad employee provided us with tea during the thirty-six hours that lay ahead for us. He also assisted us in preparing our beds in our sleeping quarters in the evening and willingly provided information about everything. In contrast, we experienced the soldiers at the border and the custom officers as extremely harsh and suspicious officials. We sensed that Poland was viewed as an unreliable partner in the Warsaw Pact by the German Democratic Republic and the Soviet Union. Both in Frankfurt on the Oder and in Brest the gun barrels were set in the direction of Poland. The Poles had attempted to go their own socialist way since 1956.

In Brest our train was transferred from the European narrow track system to the wider Russian track. We traveled through an immense, open countryside the remainder of the night and the following day. The farther east we traveled, the poorer the farm villages looked, depressed flat into the green meadows and woods. We knew about the cities like Minsk and Smolensk from the war reports before 1945. Horrible things must have occurred here during World War II. We saw Smolensk on an elevation from a great distance with the old fortress over which towered the cathedral with golden and colorful domes.

Christiane's brother Berthold welcomed us in one of Moscow's train stations. We brought our luggage to a hotel and took advantage of the warm evening for a first stroll through the old city. As we turned into the Red Square, with a view of the colorful St. Basil Cathedral and behind it the grand panorama of the Kremlin, with its churches, towers, and palaces, a carillon rang out. It was magically beautiful. We completely forgot that we were in the center of a world power.

In our continuing journey during the following days, we traveled along the Volga-Moskva Canal. During its construction many Russian convicts but also German war prisoners lost their lives. When we arrived at the Volga, we were impressed by its width and majesty. We reached the goal of our journey, the small, international city of Dubna, where the Dubna flows into the Volga. Our relatives lived here, together with Mongolians, Russians, Poles, Czechs, and citizens of other socialist countries. Their employer was the Institute of Nuclear Physics.

The Volga shore near Dubna was densely covered with vacationers every day in August. Their greatest concern seemed to be to protect their noses with newspapers against sunburn. Wagons where one could change, as we know them from pictures from the imperial times, were placed close to the water. There was busy boat traffic on the Volga. In addition to large cruise liners, small, aged passenger boats operated on the river. Among them extra-long rafts from the Valdai Hills allowed themselves to be swept down the river. They had to be divided into smaller sections near Dubna. Otherwise, they could not fit into the locks. The rafters were jaunty figures with shaggy beards and wild hair. Their faces were furrowed by wind and weather, and they were not adverse to alcohol. One day a modern hovercraft whizzed over the Volga, as if it were flying. A few days later we read in the paper that Khrushchev[1] intended to give such a boat to the British queen as a present.

We explored the nearby surroundings on foot, with bicycles, on ships, and in buses. The farmhouses here were constructed of wooden beams and adorned with beautiful decorations above the windows and doors. We discovered wells with swivel beams as long as a tree, large herds of cows and horses on the Volga meadows, few "working" churches, and many

---

1. Nikita Khrushchev (1894–1971) ruled the Soviet Union as First Secretary of the Communist Party from 1953 until 1964 and as Premier from 1958 until 1964.

dilapidated places of worship. We received the impression that the Russians lived significantly better here on the Volga than in poor Belarus.

One day we traveled on a small ship to the little country town, Kimri, that is located directly on the Volga. The German troops did not advance to this point. However, the population here was also affected by the sorrow of war. We were struck by the many war-disabled men with amputated arms and legs. They struggled on the streets without prostheses.

A funeral happened to take place in the church, after which the funeral procession went through the whole city. The women cried out with high, shrill sounds, and the men sang along with deep bass voices. All of the passersby on the street stopped and gave the deceased the last honor, some by making the sign of the cross, others with a quiet bow. The many cobbler workshops attracted our attention in the narrow streets. They were humbly located in the basements, as we knew them from the Russian literature of the nineteenth century.

We also experienced a picturesque weekly market. Abundant amounts of meat were offered, in addition to fruits and vegetables. The severed animal heads indicated whether it was veal, goat meat, or pork. One could fish out the meat one wished to purchase with long forks or hooks. On our return to the boat dock we passed inebriated people who could sleep off their intoxication on the sidewalks without disturbance.

In 1960 the huge "divine images" of communism, Lenin and Stalin, still stood on the large Moscow Sea, where the Volga is directed into the Volga-Moskva Canal. Stalin had, in fact, already been exposed as a distorter of communism by Khrushchev four years earlier. However, his monuments disappeared only gradually.

During bus trips in old, dilapidated vehicles we endured unpaved roads with deep potholes. Little carts with cute horses passed by us. Behind the neighboring forest was the Institute for Nuclear Physics in which top scientific accomplishments were achieved.

Interesting Russia, with such contradictions!

1961

The Berlin Wall

WE PACKED OUR LUGGAGE late in the evening on August 12, our third wedding anniversary. We wanted to spend our vacation somewhere along the Baltic Sea. We intended to pick up our tent from relatives in East Berlin on August 13 and then continue our travels immediately in a northerly direction.

We traveled with the first bus from Mücheln to Merseburg on August 13. We wanted to buy our tickets at the ticket counter in order to be able to travel through East Berlin. "We are sorry," said the woman railway employee. "We may not sell any tickets to Berlin." As we reacted in an alarmed and surprised manner, she asked sympathetically and compassionately—perhaps she considered us to be refugees who wanted to leave for West Germany at the last moment—"Well, then, have you not heard any of the news reports?" We asked impatiently, "What has happened?" The young woman became hesitant. She dared not reveal herself as a RIAS[1] listener to strangers. She said briefly, "I also do not know the situation precisely. There is talk about a wall. This is what the rumors indicate. However, what I do know for certain is that we are not allowed to sell any tickets to Berlin!"

At that time we did not suspect what kind of role the Berlin Wall would play in the future. Initially, we were angry because it had canceled all of our vacation plans. We could not travel to the Baltic without a tent. We

---

1. RIAS is the abbreviation of Rundfunk im amerikanischen Sektor, a radio and television station in West Berlin. It obviously provided information that was not shared by the press approved by the government of the German Democratic Republic.

booked our tickets to Wittenburg by way of Ludwigsfelde. Christiane's sister Friederike had lived there for the past two years with her young family.

After several transfers we arrived in Wittenburg in the afternoon and also quickly found the modern apartment of our relatives. They were not negatively surprised by the unannounced guests. They welcomed us warmly. We recognized immediately that we could only stay in the two-and-a-half-room apartment for one night. The young married couple was fully occupied with their firstborn daughter and needed both room and time for their parenting.

Other possibilities for overnight accommodations also emerged. Our vacation still became an interesting one, but it did not become a nice one. We followed the events in Berlin with great concern. The East-West antagonisms became sharper and more threatening. We felt this particularly intensively in our little conjugal bliss because we had known for a few days that Christiane was pregnant. We were enormously pleased by the news of our first child. However, into what kind of menacing world will the child be born? There was often talk of a third world war now. We Christians asked ourselves the anxious question, "How will things proceed with our church now?" After all, we belong to the all-German "Evangelical Church in Germany." In November 1960 the church had addressed a word to the congregations and had called on the members to remain in the German Democratic Republic. The governmental authorities responded with extreme annoyance because the church addressed a taboo topic publicly. However, many congregational members also manifested much lack of understanding. The church in the East had no more future for them. In the face of such an attitude, the bishop's letter in the year 1960 wanted to bear witness that the church has a raison d'être and a large sphere of activity even in a country with an atheistic world view. However, does this continue to be valid now after the construction of the wall?

1962

A Stormy February Night

THE NEWS ABOUT THE birth of our first child reached me at the pastors' conference. I traveled with joy to the children's hospital in Merseburg in the evening. Our firstborn—his name, Robert, had been settled for months—took his time during his birth. Christiane lay in the hospital for two days and waited for her first child. Now, of all things, it happened on the birthday of his father. Father and son would celebrate their birthdays together in the future. Everything was still so inconceivable. He looked so small and fragile as the nurse showed me the little fellow, snuggled up deeply in a large pillow. I was truly scared. Will he ever grow up? The nurse reassured me. Normal length; normal weight; all members and organs are healthy.

Christiane lay relaxed and quiet in her bed. Joy and happiness beamed from her eyes. And my wife was beautiful! I had never discerned before that my wife was so beautiful! As the nurse quietly informed me that the visitation time had ended and that mother and child now needed their rest, I embraced my wife carefully. I did not dare touch our child.

The storm outside had increased. It became colder and colder and more and more unpleasant. I was glad that the bus to Mücheln left on time. The storm howled more and more threateningly on our way through the various small towns. Full of concern, I thought about our large church roof. As I exited in Mücheln, a squall from the storm struck me. I battled the few hundred meters to the church square with difficulty. It was very dark around the whole church. I could not see any part of the roof. However, I did bump into broken shingles with my feet. I escaped into our small deaconry and immediately went to bed. I had to be rested the next morning. Various surprises would await me.

However, I could not go to sleep. My thoughts wandered to Merseburg to Christiane and to our son. They were now sheltered and provided for in the small private hospital. However, what awaited us in the next years? Universal compulsory military service was instituted in both German countries after the building of the wall. Two German armies then opposed each other. And will conscientious objectors be recognized in the East as in the West? Our firstborn will also have to make a decision when he turns eighteen years old. I wanted to calm myself with the argument, "In eighteen years; that is, after all, still a long time!"

Suddenly I heard a crackling and rumbling and splintering, and the howling of the storm became unbearable. I experienced in very near proximity how a large part of the church roof was destroyed. I lay in bed helplessly and could not take action. However, I could plan for tomorrow morning. I had to inform our roofer. He had to estimate the storm damage for the insurance and order the necessary roofing tile. Then I needed at least ten congregational members who would help me cover the most dangerous open places tomorrow afternoon with blankets and tarps, with boards and panels. Our delicate stucco ceiling over the worship space must be preserved from greater damage! I did not fall asleep again that night.

However, the next morning my initial thoughts did not revolve around the church roof. I dialed the telephone number of the Merseburg hospital and congratulated my wife on her birthday, one day after our men's birthday. I thanked her because she had presented me with such a splendid son.

1963

A Star Falls from Heaven's Vault

THE TELEPHONE RINGS IN the deaconry in Mücheln on a magnificent August morning. The maternity ward in Merseburg announces, "You will be able to greet the mother and newborn little daughter in their home in an hour." I had reckoned that this would happen a few hours later. The rose gardener from Schmirma had promised me fresh roses. I grabbed my bicycle, informed the roofers who were putting a new roof on our small parsonage that I would be away for forty-five minutes, and dashed off. I met the rose gardener in the field. He interrupted his work and, first of all, cut dark red roses for my wife. His skillful hands arranged them into a bouquet and bound them together tightly so that I could transport them securely on the bicycle. He selected pretty small pink roses for the newborn little girl and tied them to the large bouquet. He said, "The newborn belongs to the mother!" He did not want any money. "This is my present! Now go quickly!" I thanked him and rode off.

    As I turned into the church square, the roofers waved to me cheerfully and informed me by means of signals that the expected ones had already arrived. I untied both bouquets from the bicycle and stormed into the garden, a bouquet in each hand. Christiane stood there in the blooming garden with the sleeping child in her arms. I embraced both of them happily with my bouquets of roses. It was a pity that Robert, our firstborn, could not experience this as well. He had caught whooping cough while staying with the Hettstedt grandparents and had to be completely cured of it first. Just as we wanted to go into the house, the roofers came down from the roof. They wanted to have their breakfast in the garden. Embarrassed, they extended their greetings and wished the mother and child happiness and blessing.

I carried the little girl, who was to be named Sabine, in my arms up the steps. Christiane followed with both bouquets. A second little crib awaited the new arrival. The wall behind the little crib had been colorfully decorated by Christiane. A magnificent, multicolored rooster allowed himself to be admired by his hens. A delicate butterfly fluttered among flowers. A delightful, colorful children's world spread out in the nursery. A cheerful bird soared upward in the brightly colored picture and rejoiced and sang,

> When a little child is born into the world,
> a star falls from heaven's vault;
> a bush bursts open with blossoms;
> a bird flies high into the air;
> and sings with a bright spirit:
> "God's heart is great and good!"[1]

In the afternoon we await Grandmother Elisabeth from Naumburg.

---

[1]. The verse is a compilation of two stanzas, slightly revised, from a song, titled *Kommt ein Kindlein auf die Welt*, by Ruth Schaumann, (1899–1975) who was a German poet and sculptor.

1964

Construction Soldiers

COMPULSORY UNIVERSAL CONSCRIPTION WAS instituted in the German Democratic Republic on January 24, 1962 after the Federal Government had already decided to do so in West Germany on December 8, 1961. At the next opportunity we inquired of the council of the district of Merseburg when a law for the regulation of an alternative service for conscientious objectors would follow. The prompt answer was, never! We had anticipated this answer. However, then something else nevertheless happened!

In the following two years about three thousand young men refused to serve in the military. They knew what was associated with this: multiple years in prison and lasting discrimination in one's occupation. The governmental authorities did not expect such a reaction. When they realized that the ecclesiastical leaders supported the conscientious objectors with no ifs or buts[1] they felt compelled to issue an ordinance regarding the establishment of units for construction soldiers (September 7, 1964). That was a unique measure in the socialist camp. I had two young men in my congregation who declared themselves to be pacifists in 1963 and 1964, that is, before the ordinance regarding the construction soldiers was publicized. The one studied in Dresden at the Technical University, and the other had begun an apprenticeship in the brick factory in Mücheln. When the apprentice revealed to his master that he would declare himself to be a conscientious objector at the time of his conscription, the master announced that the apprentice had to discontinue his apprenticeship im-

---

1. The original reads: "... ohne Wenn und Aber..."

mediately. However, he should consider all of this one more time. He was granted a reprieve until Monday morning. I accompanied the apprentice on his difficult journey to his master on Monday. To my surprise, I was allowed to enter the factory without any question. The master hesitated when the apprentice appeared with a companion. However, since he had also brought along a colleague as a witness, he initially said nothing. The apprentice declared clearly and distinctly that he would retain his decision. The master reacted angrily and threatened that the apprentice agreement would be canceled within a few days. Then I spoke and said that a young person can, however, not be punished doubly, namely, with the cancellation of the vocational training and with imprisonment. I announced that I would immediately drive to the council of the district of Merseburg and address this matter. The master now became visibly anxious and asked me who I was. I introduced myself as the parish pastor of Mücheln. The two factory employees were left speechless. They would have preferred to scream at me or have me arrested by the factory police. However, they remained level-headed. With an ice-cold expression, they ended the conversation: "We have nothing more to say to each other."

Subsequently, I drove immediately to Merseburg and established from the council of the district, namely, the Internal Department, that the brick factory in Mücheln could not cancel the existing apprenticeship. A process against the apprentice was never initiated because the ordinance about the establishment of construction units for construction soldiers was issued in 1964. Both the student who studied in Dresden and the apprentice in Mücheln belonged to the first construction soldiers who were drafted. They belonged to that generation which prevented the employment of construction soldiers in the building of military installations, as if they were an engineer corps of the armed forces. That had to be gained arduously and resolutely and courageously. The construction units also became communities of learning as they dealt with each other. Christians of diverse confessions had to show understanding for one another. Christians and humanists had to be mutually respectful, also with regard to their varied justifications for their pacifist position.

1965

Demanding a New Eastern Policy

ON OCTOBER 15, 1965 the Evangelical Church in Germany published a memorandum on the theme "The Situation of the Refugees and the Relationship of the German People to their Eastern Neighbors." The response was a storm of indignation. The protests emanated particularly from the refugee associations: The church is abusing its authority! The memorandum is the most harmful contemporary publication! The memorandum is morally, historically, legally, and politically irresponsible!

In spite of this reaction, the synod of the Evangelical Church unanimously agreed with this memorandum on November 7, 1965. What did the Evangelical Church intend with this memorandum? It had three intentions. It wanted to set in motion the political imaginations of the citizens of the Federal Republic of Germany. It wanted to offer a free and open dialogue to the neighbors in the East. It wanted to give the politicians the courage for a new Eastern policy. All political parties initially reacted with reserve. Open, sharp attacks came from the so-called "Christian" parties. The Social Democratic Party appointed a work group that was to give the memorandum careful attention. Egon Bahr,[1] a member of the inner circle of Willy Brandt,[2] became one of the most resolute pioneers of a new political strategy toward Poland and Czechoslovakia.

   1. Egon Bahr (1922–2015) was a member of the Social Democratic Party, served as Secretary of the Chancellor's Office from 1969 until 1972, and was a chief formulator of the new Ostpolitik, or Eastern Policy, pursued by Chancellor Willy Brandt.

   2. Willy Brandt (1913–1992) led the Social Democratic Party from 1964 until 1987 and served as Chancellor of the Federal Republic of Germany from 1969 until 1974. His

Demanding a New Eastern Policy

An invitation from the Polish Roman Catholic bishops to the German Roman Catholic bishops to the millennial celebration of the Christianization of Poland on November 18, 1966 was a direct response to the memorandum of the Evangelical Church in Germany.

It still took some years on the political level. When Brandt became foreign minister in the great coalition government, he already initiated a new Eastern policy. However, he achieved the major breakthrough only as chancellor. He signed the German-Polish treaty in Warsaw on December 7, 1970. Before the signing he allowed himself to be given a tour of Warsaw. Brandt spontaneously knelt before the monument that was a reminder of the insurrection in the Warsaw ghetto. He writes about this later in his *Erinnerungen*:[3] "Under the burden of the most recent German history, I did what humans do when words fail. Thus I remembered the millions who were murdered. Whoever wished to understand me, could understand me..."

In the summer of 1965 Christiane and I were guests in the ecclesiastical retreat center Sola Fide in Janské Lázně in the Giant Mountains. We experienced lovely vacation days together with Czech pastors' families from the Evangelical Church of the Bohemian Brethren. For many Czechs it was the first time that they sat together at one table with Germans and ate and prayed with them. That was not easy for them. They had consciously experienced the war and naturally also all of the horrible things that Germans inflicted on Czechs during that time. I was glad that I was able to tell them that our Evangelical Church in Germany was preparing a memorandum that was intended to initiate a new relationship with the eastern neighbors. The theological professor Hromádka from Prague had a mountain cabin in Janské Lázně. We visited him. He had to leave his country in 1938 when the German troops marched into Prague. While in exile in the United States, he

---

birth name was Herbert Ernst Karl Frahm, but he began to use the name Willy Brandt while he worked as a journalist during the Nazi period in order to make it more difficult for Nazi agents to identify and locate him. He had fled to Norway in order to escape Nazi persecution because of his socialist leanings. He decided to use his adopted name officially in 1948. As Chancellor he strongly supported West Germany's alliance with the United States and the West, but he also implemented a new Eastern Policy with the intention of improving West Germany's relationship with the Eastern European countries. He continued to be an ardent opponent of communism, however.

3. Willy Brandt does describe this event in Brandt, *Erinnerungen*, 214. However, he does not include the words "Whoever wished to understand me, could understand me..." in his account. The same is true of the abbreviated English translation of Brandt's *Erinnerungen*. See Brandt, *My Life in Politics*, 199–200.

wrote a book with the title *Leaping over Walls with my God*.[4] (See Ps 18:29.) This book has considerably defined my way in ecclesiastical service.

---

4. See Hromádka, *Sprung über die Mauer: ein Hromádka Lesebuch*.

1966

Who Are You?

WE YOUNGER PASTORS IN the ecclesiastical district of the Geisel Valley endeavored to organize as much parish work as possible on a regional level, especially when it concerned young adults and youth. Representatives of the individual youth groups met every month in a youth meeting in the new community center in Bedra. Experiences from the congregations were exchanged and joint projects were prepared. During the winter of 1966 to 1967 we prepared a youth week, which we carried out from April 13 through 16, 1967 in Mücheln.

The general theme was: "Human being, who are you?" It was divided into three subthemes:

1. What is your true appearance? (mask or reality?) in school or vocation
2. What is your origin? (creation or evolution?)
3. What does God mean to you? (Is faith a narcotic?)

The following Bible passage was interpreted during worship: "Whoever serves me must follow me, and where I am, there will my servant be also. Whoever serves me, the Father will honor." (John 12:26 NRSV)

The privacy wall in the large parish meeting room was decorated with myriad pictures of human beings in various sizes and decorated with bright and dark masks. During the first evening a youth performed a one-person show and acted out diverse variations of human masquerades.

The theme of the youth week had provoked a stir in Mücheln. Even officials of the Free German Youth came out of curiosity. They were puzzled that so many young people allowed themselves to be addressed thematically without pressure or constraint.

There was no official connection between church and school. A few teachers belonged to the congregation, but they did not dare to be actively involved. A teacher visited me once in the evening and gave me a relatively large financial contribution. He had joined the Socialist Unity Party of Germany as a secondary school teacher and thereby also left the church at the same time. During his camping vacation on the Baltic he was delighted each time, also because he could participate in the worship service there without being recognized. He only attended the Christmas Eve service in Mücheln when the church was overcrowded. A few years prior a grandchild had lost its life in an accident. The grandfather cared for and decorated and honored the grave of the grandchild like a relic.

I had a conversation with another teacher in connection with a preparation for a funeral. He asked me whether it was acceptable that my wife had studied biology. I confirmed that it was. He could not comprehend this. Christian faith and science were incompatible for him, just like water and fire.

We had a retired secondary school teacher in our congregation who had been very active as a German Christian[1] during the time of National Socialism. Because he was no longer employed in the teaching profession, he dared open contact with the congregation. He often came to me for personal conversations. He was interested in my experiences in the Black Pump. I told him about my ideas regarding the church in a secularized world and about my inferences with regard to worship. There can no longer be a distinction between the sanctuary and the community hall. The altar belongs in the community hall. The pastor no longer wears clerical garb. The pastor is a member of the congregation like all others, only with special functions. He is an official, but not a priest. He is not a mediator between God and the people. However, then the liberal secondary school teacher protested energetically, to my surprise. The priest belongs in the congregation. The people want this. Holy space, holy liturgy, festive garb—these belong to religion! I heard similar things from my fellow workers in the Black Pump. I was disappointed.

---

1. The German Christian movement was promoted by the Nazis and consisted of people, particularly from Protestant communities, who were officially members of the churches but also supported the policies of the Hitler regime. The Bekennende Kirche, or the Confessing Church, opposed the movement and sought to be faithful to the Christian heritage by rejecting the racist ideology of the National Socialists and its consequences and by resisting Nazi interference in ecclesiastical matters.

1967

Pastor in Lutherstadt Eisleben

IN THE BEGINNING OF the year I was troubled by a rumor that I was mentioned during deliberations about the start of a congregation in the developing new city near Halle, namely, Halle-Neustadt. However, then other solutions emerged. And I was glad about it. Until that time, I had not thought about a change in my place of pastoral ministry. I was comfortable in Mücheln and saw continuing new possibilities for our work. However, once a person has become part of a conversation that person is never left in peace again. Bruno Schottstädt from the Gossner Mission offered a team ministry position in the country, in Nitzahn near Rathenow. Two pastors had begun ecclesiastical work there together in a larger area of several Agricultural Production Cooperative villages. One of the pastors left this work prematurely for personal reasons. I should now step in for him. After intensive inquiries and conversations, I declined. However, the next offer came quickly, namely, the pastorate at the St. Andrew Church in the Lutherstadt Eisleben. Provost Fleischhack[1] convinced me. After a sad farewell to the congregation in Mücheln and the ecclesiastical district of the Geisel Valley, we moved to Eisleben in September, into the old superintendent's house on the St. Andrew church square. An inscription next to the pointed entrance portal indicates to the new residents that Pastors

---

1. Heinz Fleischhack (1913–1988) became a member of the Confessing Church during the Nazi period and was significantly impacted by the theological perspectives of Dietrich Bonhoeffer and Karl Barth. He was drafted into the army and captured by the Soviets. After his release he served as a pastor in Eisleben and then as pastor and as provost in Magdeburg.

Johannes[2] and Cyriacus Spangenberg[3] lived and worked here as the first Evangelical pastors. The latter is the composer of the Easter hymn, "Now glad of heart be everyone." A dignified, large home with a long hallway and many rooms was available to us. It was cold in the winter and cool in the summer. Our children learned to ride their bikes in the home.

 A few days after our move we experienced many events related to the theme "Reformation Anniversary." Four hundred and fifty years earlier, Luther had nailed his Theses to the Castle Church in Wittenberg on October 31. Ecumenical guests from all parts of the world came: from the Scandinavian countries, from Finland, from the Balkans, from Czechoslovakia and Poland, from England and the United States of America. We constantly had overnight guests. One evening we sat in a larger reception in the Mansfelder Hof. An additional ecumenical guest from the United States arrived late. He greeted people cheerfully and lightheartedly and found an open place at the long table. I sat across from him and waved to him with my wine glass. He responded immediately, grasped his wine glass that had been filled for him quickly, and waved back. But how? I suddenly discovered that the guest from America had no arms. The sleeves of the jacket were inserted in the side pockets. Our guest had—but was this truly possible?—waved to us with his foot. He held the wine glass with his toes. In the meantime, we had all noticed this. We became embarrassed. We had brought him into an awkward situation! However, he continued to master the situation. He told us in German about his serious injury during the war. He had studied theology without arms, had established a family with four children, and considers it to be his specific mission to show other people with disabilities how one can also live a meaningful life as a person with a disability.

 Our St. Andrew Church with the three church towers was in a deplorable condition, both outside and inside. The church was used much on festival days. As the responsible pastor, I was ashamed for our church

---

 2. Johannes Spangenberg (1484–1550) earned a Master's degree at the University of Erfurt in 1511 and subsequently served as pastor and educator, particularly in Nordhausen and Eisleben. He was an eager student of Scripture and also fostered the devotional life of people by collecting and publishing hymns.

 3. Cyriacus Spangenberg (1528–1604) was the son of Johannes Spangenberg. He was educated at the University in Wittenberg and succeeded his father as pastor of the St. Andrew Church in Eisleben. As a theologian, he challenged the more conciliatory and accommodating theology of Philip Melanchthon (1497–1560) and was a proponent of Gnesio-Lutheranism. His understanding of original sin, adopted from his mentor Matthias Flacius Illyricus (1520–1575), involved him in a significant theological controversy and caused him to leave Saxony for Strasbourg.

in the presence of the many guests who came from all parts of the world. However, the governmental representatives must also have been ashamed, for how else can it be explained that, after the festivities, construction assistance in the amount of 80,000 Marks was announced for our congregation? I was given a huge task two months after I began my service.

1968

End of the Prague Spring

ON A LONG, WARM August evening in the year 1968 we sat comfortably in an ecclesiastical retreat center in Vrbno in the High Ash Mountains. Czech and German pastors made plans for the coming months. What unimagined possibilities appeared on the horizon in the land freed by the "Prague Spring"! We wanted to bring together Christians from both German countries and congregational members from Czechoslovakia for youth formation events, family gatherings, and choir tours. We went to bed very late that evening. The next day we wanted to celebrate Sabine's fifth birthday, and all Czech children were invited to the celebration! The birthday room had already been festively decorated with blooming plants and green branches.

We were awakened urgently around 6 a.m. early in the morning by loud knocking. Our Czech neighbors in the room next to ours stood crying at the door. They had heard unbelievable news on the radio. Czechoslovakia had been occupied during the night by troops of the Warsaw Pact. All of the members, except for Romania, had participated. Walter Ulbricht was supposedly one of the strongest chief instigators of this operation. We were ashamed for our country. We had great understanding for the spontaneous poster campaign: 1938/1968; Czechoslovakia was so deeply humiliated twice within thirty years.

Our Czech friends drove home immediately. They wanted to be with their congregations in this time of need. They asked that we take care of their children. We should by no means cancel the planned birthday celebration. We did them this favor, although we were not in the mood for celebrating. We played with the children and drank coffee with them. In the evening the mothers returned to their children. The fathers remained in the congregations.

We left for our return trip two days later. That became an adventure. No train ran according to schedule. The Czech rail officials gave no information to Germans. We fully understood their action.

We had a wonderful experience at the Děčín train station. We positioned ourselves on the platform with many other German families and waited for a train from Bad Schandau. Will it still come today, or tomorrow, or two days from now? Who knows?

Then a Czech woman rail official came walking on the platform and saw our two children who were lying exhaustedly and sadly on a blanket. She took a chocolate bar from her pocket, handed it kindly to the children, and hurried on. I ran after her and thanked her. She said in good German: "I know how to distinguish between such and such, between friends and enemies." As the comment slipped out, "You speak German so well," she almost whispered, "I was in a German concentration camp for three years during the war." Then she did not allow herself to be detained any longer.

Deeply impressed, I returned to my family on the platform. After a few more hours the train from Bad Schandau came and brought us to Dresden. Our German border police treated us like counter-revolutionaries. They searched our luggage for photographs, notes, and printed materials. We were welcomed by a police cordon with dogs in the Dresden railway station. Intimidated and disconcerted, we squeezed past them with our frightened children and with our luggage.

1969

Drama after Klaus's Birth

HIS BIRTH IN THE hospital of the Lutherstadt Eisleben went smoothly and without complications. I was informed about the birth in the morning, just as I was on the way to the St. Andrew Church with a group of construction experts. An extensive renovation of the church was to begin in four weeks, and much still had to be settled beforehand.

I disappeared for two hours in order to congratulate my wife and see our third child, whom we awaited with great excitement. After my return there was a big hello in the dignified church. The construction workers expressed many good wishes for the newborn Klaus. The kind Bishop Nicholas genially confirmed the good wishes from high on the medieval altar shrine of the St. Andrew Church. In one hand the patron saint of Klaus holds three golden globes. What prophecies for the newborn child will they contain?

A few days later we could pick up the mother with the child from the hospital. It was an ice-cold December day. The gas supply in the houses on the St. Andrew church square did not function anymore. We could not use our gas stove. A little electric hotplate had to suffice. Then the water line in the house froze. I began to thaw out the water pipes with an old, proven method, namely, with hot cloths. I had not made much progress when I had to interrupt. Cantor Stoll and I drove to the hospital in order to bring the new Eisleben resident, Klaus Hartmann, triumphantly into the venerable, medieval parsonage. He cooed happily with his tiny voice as we carried him up the old steps of the stairway. His siblings awaited their brother in the large nursery. They admired the little fellow as he was carefully unwrapped from the many blankets and pillows. Grandmother Elisabeth from Naumburg, who had already taken over the maintenance of the household in Eisleben several days earlier, took her twelfth grandchild into her arms with much joy.

As I turned again to the frozen water pipes, I discovered that the catastrophe was a perfect one. There was a burst water pipe in the basement. I could not turn off the water because the break had occurred before the shut-off valve. We needed an expert who could turn the water off in the street. I ran off in order to find such an artisan before our potato supply in the basement sank under the surface of the water. Finally, all dangers were averted. I looked for our Klaus. He lay satisfied and satiated in the spick-and-span little bassinet, blinked at us, and cheerfully moved his little fingers. We turned off the big light, left a faint wall light on, and snuck out of the bedroom.

Now we finally found peace after an exciting day. Grandmother Elisabeth had prepared a splendid evening meal. After half an hour Christiane once more checked on our Klaus and returned very upset. The blindingly white little children's bed was soiled with blood. Profoundly frightened, we requested an ambulance. Klaus was thoroughly examined in the hospital. The doctor reassured us. The blood did not come from the child but from the mother. A few little blood vessels had burst in Christiane's breast. The nursing baby had also drunk the mother's blood with the mother's milk. Apparently, that did not taste good to him, and he spit everything out onto the white pillow. Was that his first child's play with colors?[1] Now the evening did still become a peaceful one.

---

1. Klaus Hartmann is now a well known artist in Berlin.

1970

Adventures in Church Renovation

THE UNEXPECTED ANNOUNCEMENT OF governmental construction assistance from the Nuschke Funds[1] in November 1967 was combined with a crazy stipulation. The money had to be expended for construction by December 31, 1967. I drove unannounced to the Office for the Preservation of Monuments in Halle; had myself announced to the highest official, Mr. Berger; and, by a miracle, was immediately admitted. I was listened to incredulously, with wide-open, surprised eyes. It is true, 80,000 Marks for the St. Andrew Church was only a drop in the bucket[2] considering the condition of this church. However, Mr. Berger was immediately prepared to allow a plan for the project to be prepared. He also wanted to endeavor to apply for further monetary support. Then I could do nothing else than to promise Mr. Berger that I would endeavor to find additional financial support within the ecclesiastical realm. In fact, I had no idea how this might look practically. However, I was firmly convinced that it would succeed! The following day I contacted Mr. Bolze of the Ecclesiastical Building Authorities, Halberstadt Branch. He was highly pleased and promised such support. Together with him I arranged with a Thuringian slate roof master in the following days that he would replace our church roof next spring to the extent that the fiscal resources would allow. He dated the invoice

---

1. The Otto-Nuschke-Fonds was a governmental resource in the German Democratic Republic used to subsidize the repair of buildings that were worthy of landmark designation.

2. The original reads ". . . nur ein Tropfen auf den heissen Stein . . .," which literally means "only a drop on a hot stone."

for material and work December 1967. During the winter of 1967 to 1968 additional specialists and experts appeared, provided expert opinions, and made proposals. New damage was discovered again and again. The roof framework had to be strengthened with new beams, but who would procure the wood? Only copper gutters and copper window grates are installed in the industrial atmosphere of Eisleben. Who procures the copper? How will the heating problem be solved? A heating specialist is consulted. Must changes not also be made with the pews? It is decided that three hundred new chairs, which will be heated with low-heat electric heating plates, will be placed in the front half of the nave. However, we must buy seven kilometers of coils for the chairs with which the seats will be covered. How should the lighting of the church be solved? Should the neo-Gothic floral decorations according to motifs of Cranach[3] be preserved when the interior of the church is painted, perhaps in the chancel or on the pulpit pillar? Should the gilded rose decoration in the art nouveau style on the main altar be preserved or removed? What will happen with the pictures and the carved figures? Will we still have money for them? Must the lightning rods not also be replaced? Who procures the copper nails for the shingling of the roof? How often did we sit together with the experts? How often did the church council have to confirm plans and then possibly revise or completely change those plans after eight weeks? Often it only became apparent during the practical implementation of the work what could not be easily procured. For example, the firm could provide the radiators without difficulties during the installation of the heating system. However, particular connectors were missing when the ducts were being relocated, and we had to obtain the connectors individually from various places in the German Democratic Republic.

We emptied the church between Christmas and New Year's Eve 1969 for the work on the inside of the church. Many members of the congregation, particularly members of the youth group, accomplished this heavy work. The chairperson of the church council, master chimney sweep Bach,

---

3. The reference is likely to Lucas Cranach the Elder (1472–1553) who was a German artist and served much of his career as court painter of the Electors of Saxony. He is particularly known for his numerous portraits of German princes and leading reformers, including Martin Luther. He became a supporter of the Reformation, and his artistic works also depict theological themes characteristic of the Lutheran Reformation. Lucas Cranach the Younger (1515–1586), one of his sons, continued the stylistic legacy of his father. Another son, Hans Cranach or Johann Lucas Cranach (c. 1513–1537) was also a painter.

performed the many necessary work duties responsibly. We experienced building in a double sense: construction of the church building and community building. There were many surprises! And wonders occurred often!

1971

Ecclesiastical Tourism

THE LUTHER SITES IN the German Democratic Republic came to the attention of world Christianity again through the celebrations of the Reformation anniversary in the year 1967. And the government of our country recognized that tourists from all over the world and particularly from the western countries enriched our economic life. Hard currency is not to be despised. The tourism to the Luther sites was strictly organized. East German tour guides were trained for it. A travel program extending from Wittenberg to Eisenach, over Eisleben/Mansfeld and Erfurt, and with many other interim points was offered to the tourists. Particularly the Americans did not want to miss any Luther site, even when their stay cost many dollars.

On a Saturday morning I stood at the entrance of our church and waited for a bridal procession. At that time, a woman teacher from Moscow came with twenty Russian Young Pioneers[1] with red scarfs and asked in good German whether she could tour the church with her students. I gave permission but also pointed out that a church wedding would occur in a few minutes. The bridal procession came walking across the church square just as the teacher and her students were in the chancel admiring the medieval carved altar. The bells began to ring. I greeted the bride and bridegroom at the entrance and then we entered the church accompanied by festive organ music. As we came closer to the altar, I discovered the Moscow Pioneers

---

1. Young Pioneers was a youth organization in the Soviet Union and other communist countries, including the German Democratic Republic. Red scarfs were part of the uniform of the Soviet Young Pioneers.

positioned against the walls of the chancel. I nodded in an encouraging manner to the somewhat disconcerted teacher. Then the worship service proceeded as planned. The church door opened suddenly before the blessing of the bride and groom. A large group of American tourists pressed into the church "armed to the teeth"[2] with cameras. As they discovered the kneeling bride and groom in the chancel, our energetic sexton could no longer stop them. They pressed forward to the first rows of chairs and sat down noisily. There was flashing and cracking and clattering, and one could plainly hear their excited breathing! Then it became totally quiet. I blessed the bride and groom. We sang a cheerful hymn, and then I walked with the bridal procession to the door of the church, once again accompanied by the organ. The Russian woman teacher joined the bridal procession with her students and thanked me. We exchanged best wishes. I went back to the Americans. They now sat in their places quite devoutly and well-behaved. An American pastor embraced me and said with an emotional voice: "That it is so difficult for you." I did not understand. He explained: "That the communists do not leave you in peace even in the church." Now I understood. He was thinking of the Pioneers with the red scarfs. I could set the record straight for the whole group that this was also a group of tourists and that we often discover a great openness and attentiveness to ecclesiastical activities, particularly among visitors from the Soviet Union. I told the Americans about a group of engineering students from Georgia who insisted on entering our church in January when the temperature was twenty degrees Celsius below zero and on singing old spiritual folk songs in the chancel for an hour in harmony, together with their professor. The songs were sung at births, marriages, and funerals in the Caucasus.

The ecclesiastical tourism was often a great burden in the Luther cities. Tour groups sometimes announced themselves even at 9 p.m.! However, it was an even greater enrichment and encouragement for our congregations!

---

2. The original reads "bis an die Zähne bewaffnet."

1972

A Christian in Socialism

PROVOST DR. FALCKE[1] PRESENTED a lecture this year at a general synod of the Evangelical Church in Dresden on the theme, "Christ frees—therefore church for others." The lecture attracted much attention. The Christians in the German Democratic Republic were troubled by the question, "Do we still have a future in the German Democratic Republic after the building of the wall (1961) and after the forced ending of the Prague Spring (1968) and after the division of the Evangelical Church in Germany into an Eastern and a Western Church (1969)?" Heino Falcke answered this question with an unequivocal "yes." We have a future if we, as "church for others," know ourselves to be responsible for the people in our country and for the society. Christ does not leave our country but remains at work here and, in doing so, Christ uses His modest church. He gives us the possibility to work for a more just society and for an "improved socialism" in this place, whether our government wants this or not. The church was thereby given its assignment for the next twenty years. There was the greatest concern and doubt

---

1. Heino Falcke (b. 1929) was the director of the practical seminary of the Evangelical Church of the Union in Gnadau from 1963 until 1973 and then served as a provost in the Evangelical Church of the Ecclesiastical Province Saxony from 1973 until 1994, specifically in the Erfurt region. He was also chairperson of the Commission for Church and Society of the Confederation of Evangelical Churches in the German Democratic Republic from 1974 until 1987 and a member of the Commission for Church and Society of the World Council of Churches for a number of years, beginning in 1975. As Hartmann indicates, his presentation in Dresden attracted much attention, within both the church and the ruling political party. The latter unsuccessfully sought to prevent the distribution of the presentation.

within the church, and the government reacted angrily and sensitively. How could one speak of an "improved socialism" at a public church synod? The existing socialism of the German Democratic Republic was, after all, good!

During a weekend in September, 1972 an event for secondary school students took place in Eisleben under the theme "Being a Christian in Socialism." A group of hippies from Sangerhausen attended unannounced, and we had to engage them spontaneously. The leading figure of this group carried with him the *Meditations* of Emperor Marcus Aurelius. The peace wish "Shalom" greeted others on the back of his jacket, which was made of sheep's wool. Our youth group was challenged in a wholly new manner. Some time later we organized a youth day in Eisleben. We wanted to consider the tasks of Christians in society in various study groups. We had prepared posters for the event, which we placed in the chancel. On one poster one saw a squadron of soldiers in rank and file with rifles in their arms marching in one direction. A single person with a spade in his hand marched past them going in the opposite direction. This poster invited people to participate in the study group "Construction soldiers." A large factory door had been painted on the other poster. The door was closed and over it was the inscription "State-owned factory." Behind the door were various socialist slogans. In between was a large cross. The message of this poster was that even in a state-owned factory there is room for Christians. A similar poster invited participation in the study group, "The Christian in the School." As we prepared everything in the church on the Saturday before the youth day, a group from the Cultural Association appeared suddenly. They wanted to tour our Luther church. I invited them in a friendly manner and guided them through the church. In concluding I said a few words about the posters and drew attention to the youth day. Then I suddenly noticed stony faces on some of the visitors. I suspected something bad. The group suddenly had no more time. One visitor still whispered to me at the exit: "Good luck tomorrow. We are a group of teachers from this district." There was much telephoning in the Eisleben district that night. A Christian teacher who wanted to lead one of the study groups and several students canceled on short notice. However, the youth Sunday was held as planned.

1973

An Inter-congregational Reform Circle

THE CONTINUALLY NEW CHALLENGES faced by shrinking congregations required examination of our structures. Church leadership, synods, and working committees occupied themselves with such questions as: How many buildings can we still afford? How can the administrative work in the congregations and the circuit be improved? Could it perhaps be done by merging congregations or by developing parishes? How can pastors and catechists, who must serve more and more congregations, accomplish their work with youth and children, with young married couples, with women's circles and men's groups more effectively by functioning inter-congregationally and regionally? This also applies to bible and prayer weeks and also to worship services and congregational celebrations. And how can congregation members discern their own responsibility in the congregations more than they have so far?

In the Lutherstadt Eisleben there were at that time four congregations with four old, large church buildings and with a tendency toward lower membership among twenty thousand inhabitants and five thousand congregation members. During inter-congregational youth events, for example, during retreat times in the Mansfeld Castle, critical questions emerged among the older youth regarding the ecclesiastical praxis in our city. During a worship service on November 10 (Luther's birthday), the youth presented ten theses whose content could be reduced to one common denominator: Do we not occupy ourselves too much with the old

Luther tradition and not enough with our ecclesiastical mission in today's society? Was Martin Luther in his time not much more oriented to social challenges than we are today? These and other questions found open ears among some of the members of the congregational councils. A so-called "reform circle" formed, within which Messrs. Prohl, Bach, Pfützner, Rostalski, and Hermann (to mention just a few names) were very active. They were prominently involved in the efforts to merge the three congregations of St. Andrew, St. Nicholas, and St. Peter. They supported all inter-congregational and regional projects, including cooperation with the Roman Catholic congregation. They also negotiated with the church administration in Magdeburg when the matter of the St. Nicholas Church was addressed. With a heavy heart we relinquished it as a congregation at that time. Our negotiations with the Mansfeld collective regarding the use of the church building as a concert hall were discontinued because of the intervention of the government of the German Democratic Republic in Berlin. The activities of the women and men in the congregational councils and the district synod were strengthened through the reform circle. Women or men accepted the role of chairperson of congregational councils or the office of president of the district synod. When the new leadership structure was instituted in 1975 in the united church district of the Mansfeld territory, it was obvious to us that the president of the district synod would also participate in the weekly meetings of the superintendent and his directors of the three ministry areas.

Women and men who were members of the congregational councils very strongly supported our efforts to make the event on November 10 at the Luther statue on the marketplace, which had become quite small, into a credible, public, confessional gathering. We were able to interest the Roman Catholic congregation in participating, as well as the Evangelical congregations in the ecclesiastical district. Martin Day now always related to three Martins: St. Martin from the Middle Ages, Martin Luther from the time of the Reformation, and Martin Luther King Jr. Thereby the connection to the present was established.

1974

Local Ecumenism

WHEN I BEGAN MY service in the Lutherstadt Eisleben in the fall of 1967 I naturally made my first official visit to the Roman Catholic rectorate. I was greeted in a friendly manner but also with surprise. An Evangelical pastor finds the time during the celebrative days of the Reformation anniversary to visit a Roman Catholic pastor and to invite him to cooperate as closely as possible. It appeared that there was distrustful reticence in this relationship on both sides. However, this changed soon.

The Stations of the Cross already had been offered to youth in the Roman Catholic parish during Lent for many years. Devotional material for the Stations of the Cross was prepared at a central place every year. The material was then adapted concretely on the local level. We participated in this process from 1971. On a Sunday we walked through a region of the Mansfeld territory from one congregation to another. We were greeted by the local congregations (sometimes Evangelical and sometimes Roman Catholic), participated in a Stations of the Cross meditation, and were then sent to the next congregation in the next location. Our objective was always to connect the suffering of Jesus with the suffering of human beings of our time. A part of this was also that we imposed on ourselves a strenuous path of many kilometers.

On one Reformation Day (October 31) I was able to convince the local Roman Catholic priest to preach a sermon from the Luther pulpit in the St. Andrew Church. During the same worship service I reminded the people about Pastor Witzel[1] who was active in the St. Andrew Church

1. Georg Witzel (1501–1573) studied at the Universities of Erfurt and Wittenberg,

during the time of the Reformation. He had become Evangelical for a time, had married, and then confessed the Roman Catholic faith again. He had moved to Eisleben with his family in order to serve the small Roman Catholic congregation that was able to maintain itself there until the death of Count Hoyer.[2] During those years there was both an Evangelical and a Roman Catholic worship service every Sunday in the St. Andrew Church. Georg Witzel was among the few personalities who endeavored to preserve the unity of the church by means of serious theological work.

Four hundred and fifty years later the Second Vatican Council had awakened new hopes for the unity of the church. In 1974 the pastoral synod in Dresden adopted a document on the theme "Ecumenism in the context of the congregation." One year later we Evangelicals made this the theme of our district synod. A Roman Catholic priest presented the Dresden document to us. We heard such sentences from a Roman Catholic document with joy and hope: "The effort to manifest unity in the Christian congregations is particularly urgent among us because a division four hundred and fifty years ago began in our area, because we have common concerns and tasks as Christians of this time and world, because Christian cooperation can become a way to faith for others." We met at so many events that I sometimes no longer knew precisely whether he or she was Roman Catholic or Evangelical. An ecumenical wedding in the St. Andrew Church caused a stir because, through efforts that took several weeks, we were able to win the approval of both Magdeburg bishops to celebrate the Eucharist in a worship service with Evangelicals and Roman Catholics.

When I left Eisleben two Roman Catholic parishioners independently gave me their hymnbook. I was deeply impressed.

---

was ordained in 1520, and was impacted by the Lutheran reform movement. He married and continued his studies while serving as a parish pastor. His academic pursuits convinced him that Lutheran theology, including Lutheran ethics, was not a faithful expression of the Christian heritage. The essential role of good works in the Christian life was of particular interest to Witzel. He returned to the Roman Church in 1533, published various works, and sought to promote the reunification of the Western Christian community by pointing to the early church as a model for unity. When his efforts were unsuccessful, he devoted himself to defending Rome and its teachings.

2. Count Hoyer VI (1477–1540) of Mansfeld was an opponent of the Reformation, a loyal ally of Emperor Charles V (1500–1558), and a defender of Rome.

1975

The Peasants' War

AN EVENT SPONSORED BY the Cultural Association on this theme had occurred already in the fall of 1967 in Eisleben. Various participants in the discussion requested that historians and theologians dialogue with one another in a timely manner, for Thomas Müntzer was, after all, not only a revolutionary but also a theologian who derived his social ideas from the bible. After the event, I was invited to join a local philosophical study group by a teacher in an extended secondary school. The study group met monthly and philosophized with one another in a free, independent manner—that was particularly emphasized!—regarding the theme "God and the world." I was completely surprised and accepted initially on a trial basis. We then met regularly for a whole year, prepared short papers, and discussed them. "We" consisted of several teachers of the extended secondary school, a medical doctor, and I as theologian. I described in one contribution how the theologian Karl Barth[1] appreciated Ludwig Feuerbach[2] as

---

1. Karl Barth (1886-1968) was a Swiss Reformed theologian who made a profound impact on Christian theology during the twentieth century. He rejected both the liberal theology dominant in Germany and liberal theology's conservative critics. His own study of Scripture, particularly St. Paul's Epistle to the Romans, inspired him to forge his own theological path by promoting what has been described as dialectical or neo-Orthodox theology, which was significantly impacted by the heritage of Jean Calvin (1509-1564). He was teaching in Germany when Adolf Hitler came to power, opposed the rise of the Nazis, strongly supported the Confessing Church, and was the chief author of the Barmen Declaration in 1934. Because he refused to pledge loyalty to Hitler, he was compelled to resign his professorship at the University of Bonn in 1935. He then returned to Switzerland and served as professor at the University of Basel for the remainder of his career.

2. Ludwig Feuerbach (1804-1872) was a German philosopher and anthropologist.

theologian and philosopher. When an ice-cold winter descended on the Prague Spring on August 21, 1968, the philosophical circle also ended immediately in Eisleben.

However, within the church, also in our local context, we occupied ourselves extensively with the subject matter "Church and Revolution," Martin Luther and Thomas Müntzer. We also visited the Thomas Müntzer sites: Stollberg; Allstedt; Heldrungen; Bad Frankenhausen; and the Schlachtberg[3] on the Kyffhäuser Mountains, where the huge flower bed with the painting by Tübke[4] was later erected. Many scholarly works were also written during these years, and theologians and historians learned to relate to one another.

On Whit Monday in 1975 a large Free German Youth meeting took place in Eisleben. In the afternoon a large number of young people sat bored on the market square. Then Cantor Stoll and I had the idea to open our church wide, to invite the young people with organ music, and to engage them in conversation. And it worked wonderfully. Suddenly the church was blue, not from cigarette smoke, but from the blue shirts. I had also quickly found a few conversation partners. While the organ continued to play, we offered tours of the church. We discussed the topic "Church and Revolution" at the monument of Count Ernst II, who allowed Thomas Müntzer to be executed. At the monument of Countess Dorothea of Solms, who prevented a pogrom of Jews in Eisleben, we discussed anti-Semitism. At the grave of Count Hoyer we addressed the question "Roman Catholics and Evangelicals." We had displayed a number of old books in the tower library,

---

As a young man, he had intended to serve in the church. However, his university studies awakened an interest in philosophy, especially the dialectical perspective of Georg Wilhelm Friedrich Hegel (1770–1831). He then became a philosophical critic of Christianity and its chief theological assertions. He expressed that critique particularly in his 1841 volume, *Das Wesen des Christentums* (*The Essence of Christianity*). While he did not reject the existence of God, he related God's existence intimately to humanity's existence. His perspective is, therefore, anthropocentric rather than theocentric.

3. Hartmann calls it Schlachtenberg. It is an elevation near Bad Frankenhausen in Germany. The last battle of the Peasants' War of 1525 was fought there, during which Müntzer and the peasants were defeated by the forces of the princes.

4. Werner Tübke (1929–2004) was one of the most important artists in the German Democratic Republic and a member of the "Leipzig School." He is best known for the panoramic painting of the Peasants' War to which Hartmann refers.

among them the *Sachsenspiegel*[5] by Eike von Repkov.[6] We discussed legal questions. We experienced how quickly one comes to speak about contemporary problems in such an old church with art pieces from various centuries. In the following years we endeavored to keep the church open every day for a few hours, if at all possible. Congregation members were also found who provided supervision and were able to answer questions during those times. At that time young people, particularly students from the engineering school, discovered the organ music. Every organ concert was well attended. The visitors sat quietly and meditatively and allowed the beautiful church space to affect them. We experienced young people who grew up without an ecclesiastical tie to be people who were searching, questioning, curious, disappointed, and disconcerted.

---

5. The *Sachsenspiegel* is the most important collection of Saxon or Germanic customary law. This legal system remained influential for many centuries in German territories.

6. Eike von Repkov (c.1180–c.1233) was the compiler of the *Sachsenspiegel* and also translated it into Middle Low German from the Latin. The translation is one of the first literary works produced in that language.

1976

The Beacon from Zeitz

As a synodical member of the church governing body in Magdeburg I received a telephone invitation on Thursday to a special meeting that was scheduled for Saturday. On August 18 one of our pastors, Oskar Brüsewitz[1] from Rippicha, had poured gasoline on himself and set himself on fire on the market square in Zeitz after the placement of two posters. At the time he was lying in a special clinic in Halle with terrible burns, guarded against any visits by employees of the State Security Service.

I learned more details in Magdeburg. Ms. Brüsewitz and her daughter were constantly interrogated by the State Security Service. The press, managed by the state, spoke about the "action of a sick person" on Friday. Two pastors, who claimed to be friends of Brüsewitz, had acknowledged the desperate act of Oskar Brüsewitz on ARD television[2] on Friday but had remained silent about the fact that they already had requests for their departure to the Federal Republic of Germany in process for some time.

---

1. Oskar Brüsewitz (1929–1976) pursued his profession as a cobbler for a time but sought to become a pastor after his conversion to Christianity about 1954. He was able to study at a seminary in Erfurt from 1964 until 1969 and was ordained in 1970. He subsequently served a congregation in Rippicha and protested the discrimination of the political authorities in the German Democratic Republic against the church. His self-immolation was inspired by his desire to make a bold witness against oppression and for religious freedom.

2. The Arbeitsgemeinschaft der öffentlich-rechtlichen Rundfunkanstalten der Bundesrepublik Deutschland (ARD) or "Consortium of Public Broadcasters in Germany" is the organization that unites Germany's various regional radio and television broadcast institutions.

After a few days they reached their goal. They were allowed to leave and established a "Brüsewitz Center" in Bavaria,[3] which was never recognized by the church, but which played an infamous role in the political battles of the cold war.

Our bishop, Dr. Krusche,[4] who had always advocated personally on behalf of Oskar Brüsewitz when he provoked the anger of the governmental authorities because of spectacular actions, was in Tanzania at the time. His representative, Provost Bäumer,[5] wanted to prepare a "Word to the Congregations" with us which was to be distributed that night to all pastors of the ecclesiastical province (from the Altmark[6] to Erfurt) and read in all worship services on Sunday. We had to take into consideration two chief concerns in this letter. First, Oskar Brüsewitz understood all of his actions and surely also his self-immolation in front of the St. Michael Church in Zeitz as a service of witness. He wanted to be a witness of Jesus Christ and wanted to denounce injustice. The police had confiscated the two posters prepared and placed by Brüsewitz and had never shown them to representatives of the church. According to reports from eyewitnesses the text supposedly read something like this: "The churches indict communism because of its oppression of the youth." Secondly, the congregations also had to be told that God does not require such self-sacrifice from his witnesses. After all, we had to fear that this self-immolation could be imitated by others.

During the meeting of our church governing body we learned that one hundred young Marxists had expressed themselves in a declaration against the defaming articles regarding Oskar Brüsewitz in *Neues Deutschland*.

Pastor Brüsewitz died in the clinic on Sunday, August 22. The funeral service occurred on August 26 in Rippicha. There were supposedly about four hundred participants, among them about one hundred men and women pastors in clerical garb, also Roman Catholic priests. The ARD

---

3. The Brüsewitz-Zentrum was established in Bad Oeyenhausen, Westphalia, not in Bavaria.

4. Werner Krusche (1917–2009) was a German Evangelical theologian, pastor, and bishop. After his theological studies he served as a parish pastor, as director of the seminary in Lückendorf, as a theological professor in Leipzig, and as bishop of the Evangelical Church of the Church Province Saxony from 1968 until 1983. As bishop, he was a proponent of the peace movement in the German Democratic Republic and defended the church against the oppressive policies of the government.

5. Provost Bäumer's full name was Friedrich-Wilhelm Bäumer.

6. The Altmark is a region in the northern parts of Saxony-Anhalt.

correspondent, Lothar Loewe, recorded everything. The previous day the village population had been intimidated and implored by the State Security Service not to participate in the funeral service. During the celebration in the church there were, indeed, only a few faithful ones from the village present. All others came from outside the village. As we subsequently gathered at the grave near the cemetery wall and the bells rang, women and men suddenly came running from all of the homes, from the barns, from the offices, from the stores and workshops. They lined up in work clothes, crowded densely against the wall, and thus said farewell to their pastor. That was a courageous witness!

1977

A Congregation of Actors

For centuries the residents of the Mansfeld territory have celebrated the Eisleber Wiese annually in September. It is regarded as the largest folk festival of central Germany and developed from a medieval oxen market. Many entertainers travel to the area from all directions with their lottery and shooting booths; with their large and small carousels, cabin swings, and haunted amusement rides; with their supplies of cotton candy, sweets, gingerbread, and candied apples; with bratwurst stands and beer tents; and with additional items like balloons, arcade games, and fun-house mirrors in which one sees oneself wide, narrow, short, and tall. Two deacons of the Evangelical Church had already alerted us years ago to the entertainers and their families who travel from place to place with children of preschool and school age and with employees and assistants who often come from difficult social circumstances. Thus it happened that we offered one event for the entertainers and their families and another for the employees on two evenings before the beginning of the Eisleber Wiese. We always began with a devotion in the church. Then we viewed a piece of art from the church and occasionally also both the inside and outside of the organ or the St. Andrew library with its manuscripts. Subsequently, we had supper together and conversed and shared much. Of course, slides were also shown each time of other fairgrounds, also from previous years. Childcare was also organized, either in family homes or in our kindergarten. Baptisms for the children of entertainers, during which the parents sometimes also allowed themselves to be baptized, were particular high points. The deacons appeared in colorful robes during the worship services.

The Quest for Faithfulness

The entertainers and their families lived in comfortably furnished trailers. They placed value on being regarded as business people who often had been involved in their travels as entertainers to the third or fourth generation. They did not want to be confused with the "itinerant people." They understood the Romani people to be among them but also their employees, whom they had hired somewhere during their travels and who also generally disappeared again after a short time. The entertainers often simply provided a bed for them in one of the wagons carrying their materials.

The more we were challenged to open ourselves to the outside as a congregation, the more I learned to value the fact that we had a multi-talented church musician in cantor Werner Stoll who could use the organ, choirs, and instrumental groups to motivate children, youth, and adults; people who were part of the inner congregational circle, but also marginal groups or those who had no connection to the church, to participate. Our worship services were enriched musically in diverse ways, and the major oratorio performances (sometimes twice a year!) were cultural highlights, not only for Eisleben but for the whole Mansfeld region. Everything was organized in such a manner that women and men from even the smallest village congregations could attend our concerts.

All of this was happening during a time when the mood regarding domestic affairs became more and more tense. A few weeks after the death of Oskar Brüsewitz the singer Wolf Biermann[1] was deprived of his citizenship by the German Democratic Republic against his will. Seventy writers and actors and other artists from the German Democratic Republic protested against this decision. Ecclesiastical spaces were discovered as places of freedom where one could discuss all problems openly.

---

1. Karl Wolf Biermann (b. 1936) is a German singer, songwriter, and poet known particularly for his folk songs and political ballads. He was significantly impacted by the communist perspectives of his mother and by the loss of his Jewish father, who was executed in Auschwitz. He moved from the German Federal Republic to the German Democratic Republic because of his socialist perspectives. However, he was not welcomed by the communist authorities and was refused membership in the Socialist Unity Party of Germany, apparently because he was suspected of using drugs. His citizenship was revoked by the government while he was on a concert tour in West Germany.

1978

To Halle as Superintendent

A DELEGATION FROM HALLE appeared in Eisleben in February. Commissioned to do so by an election committee, they inquired whether I would be prepared to become a candidate in the election of a new superintendent for Halle. There was already a candidate from Halle. However, there was the desire to have another candidate for the selection process. After a long conversation I requested time for consideration. Much had to be considered. The new assignment attracted me, especially since Halle had already practiced the new management structure for quite some time, namely, superintendent, three leaders of specific fields of service, and a president of the synod. In the Mansfeld region we had only begun with this structure in 1975. However, I was anxious about the large city of Halle. Are the ecclesiastical conditions not unmanageable? Can a community ever grow there among the staff members and between the congregations and the regions?

And then there was an additional problem. It was still completely unclear in which congregation I would work as pastor and where our family would live. It was supposed to be in one of three congregations, Trotha,[1] St. Paul, and St. Bartholomew. The fall of 1978 was a favorable time for a move for our older children. Robert could begin his apprenticeship as cabinetmaker in Halle, and a new chapter would also begin for Sabine, if she were admitted to the expanded secondary school. However, for Klaus it would be a significant interruption. He would enter the third grade in

---

1. Trotha is a district in the northern part of Halle.

the fall. He would lose good friends in Eisleben. How quickly would he acclimate to a school in a large city?

On the other hand, we considered that we had been in Eisleben for eleven years and that it could also be good for our children to acquire a broader horizon in all directions. We finally decided for Halle. Now it became exciting: introduction to the election committee and the district synod and conversation with the church leadership in Magdeburg. Finally it was decided. I was elected. In the fall, we moved into a nice apartment on the fourth floor of a building on the Rathenauplatz in Halle, with a view of the Paulusberg with our St. Paul Church.

In March 1978 the conversations between Bishop Schönherr and Erich Honecker awakened new hopes for the relationships between government and church. Sabine's application for a place in the expanded secondary school had been denied. After the conversation on March 8, the denial was changed into an approval. We breathed a sigh of relief. Nevertheless, there was still an unpleasant surprise before the summer vacation. In a parents meeting of the eighth grade we were informed that there would be a required subject for our children beginning with the ninth grade. It will supposedly be called military education. Field exercises and target practice will be part of this instruction. I was horrified and protested and appealed to the parents that they should not allow themselves to be blindsided. That was my last appearance in a school in Eisleben. However, it was clear to me that this subject would still occupy us often in Halle.

A few days after our move we were occupied with a legal process in Halle against a woman and one of her sons. We were acquainted with them from Eisleben. They had made a request to emigrate. As convinced communists, the woman had moved to the German Democratic Republic with her husband from the Ruhr region. That was twenty years ago. In the meantime they were deeply disappointed. Because the woman was not given permission to visit her sick father, a communist who had suffered much during the Nazi period, she together with her son had publicly denounced the conditions in the German Democratic Republic in a police station. They were being sentenced for this!

1979

Halle is Better than Its Reputation

ON THE RATHENAUPLATZ WE lived on a green island in a gray, dilapidated city. We looked at the green Paulusberg that was sometimes covered with snow in the winter and attracted children and young people by the hundreds for sledding. However, we also looked at defective roofs and broken rain gutters as far as we could see. We experienced how porous our own roof was during rainy weather. The whole inner city gradually deteriorated. New neighborhoods developed at the edge of the city: Halle-Neustadt, Südstadt, Wörmlitz-Böllberg, and Silberhöhe. When we left Halle in 1986 a fourth large new area developed near Lettin. The deterioration of the inner city continued. However, the people of Halle did not become resigned. In our congregations, but also outside the church, people became self-aware and opposed the trend. People from Halle-Neustadt looked for abandoned apartments in the Paulusviertel and began to renovate them. Young people occupied houses that were supposed to be torn down, stretched tarps over the defective roofs, and fought to save them.

On the other hand, people became creative in the newly built areas in order to free the individual families from their isolation. In the congregations in the newly built areas, groups met in homes long before parish houses or churches could be built. In Silberhöhe Christmas was celebrated at a large bonfire in the open before an old village church could be renovated. I fought for a parish house for Silberhöhe for eight years against the opposition of the Socialist Unity Party of Germany on all levels. The house could be consecrated only after the Wende.

The Quest for Faithfulness

A very sensitive, lively, open-minded population lives in Halle who also did not retreat from difficult tasks in times of crisis. The controversial monument with the clenched fists on the Thälmannplatz should just be left standing. There were opposition, revolts, and insurrections against injustice and tyranny during every century in Halle. During the time of the Reformation, the citizens of Halle succeeded in driving Cardinal Albrecht[1] from the Moritzburg.[2] The people of Erfurt were not able to do this! The people of Halle always stood at the forefront when it came to such causes as the rights of the citizens, or the prerogatives of the artisan guilds, or special privileges of the people of Halle, or broken promises to students, or the eight-hour work day, or the salary demands of workers. That also applied to June 17, 1953, to the actions related to the movement "Swords to Plowshares," or to the political Wende in 1989. The history of the university, the Leopoldina,[3] the Francke Foundations,[4] the Burg Giebichenstein,[5] the Moritzburg, the theaters (including the New Theater), and many schools and other cultural and social institutions must also be acknowledged in this context. Halle is truly better than its reputation!

---

1. Albrecht of Brandenburg (1490–1545) served as archbishop of Magdeburg from 1513 until 1545 and as archbishop of Mainz from 1514 until 1545. As the latter, he was also functional primate of the churches in Germany. Martin Luther's challenge of the indulgence system in the 95 *Theses* was also a challenge of the archbishop, who fostered the sale of indulgences and benefited fiscally from that sale. Albrecht was elevated to the cardinalate in 1518. As archbishop of Mainz he was also one of the imperial electors.

2. The Moritzburg was the residence of the archbishops of Magdeburg from 1503 until Cardinal Albrecht abandoned the castle during the Reformation. It is now the home of the art museum of Saxony-Anhalt.

3. The Leopoldina refers to the Deutsche Akademie der Naturforscher Leopoldina or the German Academy of Natural Scientists Leopoldina, which is located in Halle. It was renamed the German National Academy of Sciences Leopoldina in 2008.

4. The Francke Foundations are named after August Hermann Francke (1663–1727), an important leader of the Pietist movement in Germany. Under his leadership the Pietists established an orphanage, a school, a pharmacy, and a printing house in Halle. Because of Francke's impact, the University of Halle also became an important training center of missionaries who ministered in various parts of the world, including India and Colonial North America. The printing house produced numerous bibles in various languages and greatly facilitated the dissemination of the bible throughout the world. The Francke Foundations continue to foster education, scholarship, and youth ministry.

5. The Burg Giebichenstein is a castle in Halle that was the residence of the archbishop of Magdeburg from 1302 until 1503. It is now a campus of the Burg Giebichenstein art school and is also used by the Academy of Arts in Halle.

Halle is Better than Its Reputation

Our congregations and the varied ecclesiastical institutions lived and worked in this society that was shaped in this manner and that was open to all sides. Officially, the ruling Socialist Unity Party of Germany controlled everything in the society. This did not become clearer with the constantly repeated assertion during every encounter with us: "We point out that the question of power has been clarified. This cannot be discussed!" Free spaces are also found in a totalitarian state when human beings have preserved their independence and courageously and resolutely make their own, independent decisions.

1980

A Delegation to Canada

IN THE SPRING OF 1979 the United Church of Canada invited a delegation of the Evangelical Church of the Union from the German Democratic Republic to visit Canada. The church chose the three theologians: Dr. Forck,[1] general superintendent of Cottus; Pastor Schorlemmer,[2] lecturer at the Preacher's Seminary in Wittenberg; and me from Halle for this visit. In addition, the church also chose Dr. Romberg,[3] a mathematician

    1. Gottfried Forck (1923–1996) earned a doctorate in Heidelberg after service in the military and a time as prisoner of war. After two pastorates, he served as director of the seminary in Brandenburg from 1963 until 1973, as general superintendent of the Cottbus diocese from 1973 until 1981, and as bishop of the Evangelical Church in Berlin-Brandenburg in the German Democratic Republic from 1981 until 1991. As bishop he particularly defended young people who were supporters of the peace movement in East Germany. He also challenged the political leaders to promote the democracy movement before and immediately after the Wende.

    2. Friedrich Schorlemmer (b. 1944) studied theology at the Martin Luther University Halle-Wittenberg and then served as a campus pastor in Merseburg, instructor at the seminary in Wittenberg, preacher of the Castle Church in the city, and dean of the Evangelical Academy Sachsen-Anhalt. During the time of the German Democratic Republic he was a persistent opponent of the communist regime and worked diligently for peace, for human rights, and for the protection of the environment. He was particularly active in the "Swords to Plowshares" movement. After the fall of the Berlin Wall, he opposed the reunification of East and West Germany because he envisioned East Germany as a "socialist alternative" to the Federal Republic of Germany.

    3. Walter Romberg (1928–2014) studied chemistry and mathematics and earned a doctorate at the Humboldt University in Berlin in 1954. Although he was a mathematician at the Academy of Sciences in the German Democratic Republic and chief editor of the *Zentralblatt für Mathematik*, he was an active layperson in the Evangelical Church

from Berlin. We were to become acquainted with the life of this largest Evangelical church in Canada and establish contacts between their and our congregations. Our church authorities requested the necessary travel documents. The trip was authorized for us three theologians. Dr. Romberg was denied permission. We theologians responded by returning our passports. In addition, we declared that we would only travel if Dr. Romberg could also come with us. The trip, planned for the fall of 1979, was postponed for an undetermined time. The governmental authorities reacted angrily and the ecclesiastical departments in a resigned manner. We delegates gave up all hope. To the surprise of all us the trip with us four delegates did still happen. We traveled from March 4 until April 2, 1980. We spent the first five days in Toronto. We were distributed among individual families in order to accustom ourselves to the English language. No one knew a word of German in my host family. From the very first hour I had to communicate with my school English without any experience in speaking the language. It was terrible but beneficial. During the last nights of our Canada trip I spoke English in my dreams. In those first days we became acquainted with the constantly growing city of Toronto with its three million inhabitants. One third of the inhabitants are apparently of Asian heritage and one third are people of color. Much is being done in the congregations of the United Church in order to achieve the integration of the immigrated expatriates. Congregations make sponsorship agreements. In those agreements they commit themselves to guarantee the expatriates lodging for a specific time, to find work for them, and to provide language instruction. We were welcomed by the church leadership and learned a variety of things about the history and structures of this church.

Then we traveled through the tremendously large country by car, plane, or train. Dr. Forck and I traveled through the provinces of Ontario and Nova Scotia and Dr. Romberg and Pastor Schorlemmer through Manitoba and Saskatchewan. We were in a different congregation every day; were always guests of private families for the night; experienced the congregations on weekdays and on Sundays; participated in church festivals and synodical meetings; visited reservations of indigenous people and church-related colleges and universities; were impressed by rocky promontories on the Atlantic coast of Nova Scotia, by Niagara Falls, and by interesting

---

with particular interest in the peace movement. He was also a member of the Evangelical Research Academy. He served as Minister of Finance for the East German government during negotiations leading up to the reunification of Germany.

coastal landscapes on Lake Ontario. At the conclusion, we met again in Toronto, experienced an additional synod there, and were bid good-bye with a Eucharistic celebration.

    Canadian friends asked us repeatedly whether the State Security Service of the German Democratic Republic would keep us under surveillance during this trip or whether perhaps one of us four had accepted this assignment. Such questions upset me deeply. However, I could understand them. I am still convinced now that none of us four had such an order, but that our trip was, nevertheless, watched. I was surprised by how much propaganda material of the German Democratic Republic I came across, even in Canadian congregations. And, after the opening of State Security Service files, I know now how foreign relationships on the part of pastors were watched.

1981

On the Way Together

AS REPRESENTATIVES OF THE local ecumenical community, Pastor Dr. Harold of the Roman Catholic neighboring congregation and Pastor Greif of the Evangelical Free Church (Baptists) had greeted me at my installation as superintendent in the fall of 1978. In the following years a close collaboration developed between us. Together we felt that we had been sent into the secularized city of Halle by the Lord of the church in order to bear witness to reconciliation, justice, and hope here. We celebrated many worship services together with the Roman Catholic Holy Cross congregation. On Reformation Day the Roman Catholic congregation regularly invited its Evangelical neighboring congregations to the Holy Cross Church, and we pondered together what should be reformed in our churches today. From 1985 the Roman Catholic congregation came to the St. Paul Church on Good Friday at 3 p.m., the hour of Jesus's death. We celebrated a worship service that focused on the veneration of the cross. I remember ecumenical worship services with the Roman Catholic congregation and with Orthodox congregations from Leipzig or Dresden. A joint concluding devotional service with Philipp Potter[1] in the St. Paul Church with the Free

---

1. Philip Alford Potter (1921–2015) was born in Dominica, West Indies and became a Methodist pastor who served for a time in the Caribbean and then as a staff member of the Methodist Missionary Society in London. In 1954 he joined the staff of the World Council of Churches in Geneva, with a focus on youth ministry. From 1960 until 1968 he was chairperson of the World Student Christian Federation and from 1972 until 1984 he served as general secretary of the World Council of Churches. He was awarded an honorary doctorate by the theological faculty of the University of Uppsala in

The Quest for Faithfulness

Church congregation from Ludwig Wucherer Street and with the Roman Catholic congregation from Gütchen Street in the Luther year 1983 was particularly impressive.

We did not indulge in any illusions. We complained loudly that we still could not officially celebrate Jesus's Supper together and named this a scandal. However, we also bore witness publicly to what already united us: for example, baptism. As an Evangelical pastor I baptized the child of a Roman Catholic family in a Roman Catholic worship service. I did not slip away into some niche during the subsequent celebration of the mass but prayed a prayer of lament in which I called attention to the painful separation at the table of the Lord.

We worked together theologically during joint assemblies and during meetings of our church councils: for example, before the ecumenical conference[2] in Vancouver. We jointly completed the regional history of our congregations and did not conceal at which opportunities they had failed miserably. However, we also discovered examples of courageous witnessing. In May 1985 we participated in two walks of the Stations of the Cross, one in the Getraude Cemetery and the other in the South Cemetery, as a remembrance of the conclusion of the war forty years earlier. We held devotions at individual stations: at graves of soldiers from both World Wars; at the memorial stones of the bombing victims; at the Jewish cemetery; and also at the sites of remembrance of those Germans and foreigners murdered in Halle, among them the three Roman Catholic priests Carl Lampert,[3] Herbert Simoleit,[4] and Friedrich Lorenz.[5] Only a few meters

---

1984 in recognition of his diverse ecumenical contributions.

2. Hartmann is likely referring to the sixth Assembly of the World Council of Churches that met in Vancouver, British Columbia, Canada in 1983.

3. Blessed Carl Lampert (1894–1944) was an Austrian Roman Catholic priest who opposed the Nazis during World War II. While serving as pro-vicar of the Diocese of Innsbruck he was arrested and imprisoned in the Dachau and Sachsenhausen concentration camps. Although released after eight months, he remained under surveillance while he served as a pastor and hospital chaplain in Stettin. After his second arrest in 1943, he was tortured, found guilty of treason and sedition, and ultimately executed. He was beatified by the Roman Catholic Church in 2011 for his faithful witness and ministry.

4. Herbert Simoleit (1908–1944) was a German Roman Catholic priest. While serving as a chaplain in Greifswald and Stettin, he was arrested because of his pastoral care of opponents of the Nazi regime. He himself also resisted the perspectives and policies of National Socialism. He was executed together with Carl Lampert and Friedrich Lorenz.

5. Friedrich Lorenz (1897–1944) was a German Roman Catholic priest and a

away, we discovered the grave of the armed forces judge, Werner Lueben.[6] He was a conscious Evangelical Christian who committed suicide so that he would not have to pronounce capital punishment on the three priests. The Stations of the Cross group at the Getraude Cemetery ended its walk at the group of figures created by the sculptor Horn.[7] The artist called his work "The endless street." An endless street full of suffering and tears and dread that reaches into our time becomes visible. As Christians we consciously join in the discipleship of our Lord: "He calls us outside the gates of the world. For the one who chooses his crib outside and dies outside on the field of the skull will be outside. He calls us outside the gates of the world: 'take responsibility for those outside.'" (Gottfried Schille)[8]

---

member of the Missionary Oblates of Mary Immaculate. He served as a soldier in World War I and as a military chaplain in World War II and received the Iron Cross for his bravery during both tours of duty. After his ministry as military chaplain, he was a priest in Schwerin. He was arrested by the Nazis, accused of assisting the enemy and listening to enemy broadcasts, found guilty, and executed.

6. Werner Lueben (1894–1944) was trained as a lawyer and functioned in various branches of the military legal system. He eventually was a member of the Reichskriegsgericht, the highest military court, and was appointed its chairperson on January 1, 1944. In this position, Lueben had to approve all capital punishment verdicts. He committed suicide in July 1944. His reason for doing so is still unclear, although it may be related to the sentencing of the three priests identified in the previous footnotes. Lueben had expressed his conviction that there was no valid evidence to support the verdict of capital punishment against the priests. Whether his own conscience struggles were the reason for his suicide remains unclear, however. Hartmann was obviously convinced that this was, in fact, the case.

7. Paul Horn (1876–1959) was a German sculptor who resided in Halle from 1901 until 1934 and taught and pursued his artistic labors there. When he was intensely criticized by the Nazis, he decided to leave Halle and move to Greifswald in 1934.

8. Gottfried Schille (1929–2005) was an Evangelical pastor and New Testament scholar who served much of his pastoral ministry in Borsdorf, near Leipzig. During his ministry pursuits, he published various scholarly works. There is some evidence that he also taught New Testament studies in the Theological Seminar in Leipzig. The quotation is the third verse of a hymn written by Schille based on Hebrews 13:12 and titled *Wir ziehen vor die Tore der Stadt, der Herr ist nicht mehr fern*.

1982

Swords into Plowshares

SINCE 1980 THE PEACE decade[1] has been opened in Halle with a "bridge worship service." Isaac Newton is supposed to have said, "Human beings build too many walls and too few bridges." The first year the youth went over the Giebichen stone bridge to the Kröllwitzer Church after a worship service in the St. Bartholomew Church. In 1981 the bridge worship service began in the St. Lawrence Church. The participants were youth and young families with children but also older members of the congregation. They walked through dark streets without candles and without posters to the St. Bartholomew Church and from there on to the Kröllwitzer Church. They carried the emblem "Swords into Plowshares" as a patch on their jackets. The governmental authorities reacted extremely nervously. Hundreds of employees of the State Security Service were on duty. During the devotions

1. The ecumenical Friedensdekade or "peace decade" is given this name because it lasts ten days. It is observed in Germany during the ten days before the day of repentance and prayer. The latter is typically scheduled on November 21 but has also been celebrated on other dates in November. The peace decade was fostered particularly by the youth ministry of the Evangelical Church in the German Democratic Republic, and it was publicly promoted with the theme and the emblem "Swords into Plowshares." The Roman Catholic Church and various independent churches eventually also supported this event. The government ardently opposed the peace decade and considered it to be a threat, particularly because events and conversations that addressed a variety of concerns related to life in East Germany were part of the peace decade. Because it scheduled and supported the peace decade, the church was viewed as an advocate of prayer, conversation, hope, and peace by many Christians and other residents of the German Democratic Republic. The peace decade in East Germany inspired interest among ecumenical communities throughout the world, and it has also been commemorated in West Germany since 1980.

in the three churches we also read a word regarding the events in Poland that our provincial synod adopted the previous day. After the peace decade, all of our explanations regarding the emblem "Swords into Plowshares" during conversations with the Division for Internal Affairs of the city council and with the district were not helpful. The police began an unprecedented pursuit of young people who wore the patch. On April 7, 1982 the pastoral association composed a petition to the highest police authorities in Halle and requested a suspension of the activity against young people who wore these patches. A private conversation between me and the highest police chief of Halle took place. I was assured that the governmental authorities were not interested in an escalation of this conflict. However, nothing changed. After the Wende I read a detailed record of this conversation in my State Security Service file, "Strategic Proceedings Trend," with the comment at the conclusion: "The overwhelming part of the statements of Hartmann was recorded on tape during the conversation."

In the following years we expanded the bridge worship service at the beginning of the peace decade further and further throughout the whole city. It became a simultaneous event. Devotions began at the same time in four churches (Halle-Neustadt, Kröllwitz, St. Paul, and Luther). The participants were sent in the direction of the city center, made a stop on their way in a Roman Catholic or Evangelical or Free Church congregation, and then met together for a concluding worship service in the Evangelical Market Church or in the Roman Catholic St. Maurice Church. In 1985 there were about two thousand participants in the concluding worship service.

The content of the individual stops was planned by men and women pastors, youth workers, and women and men from the various peace and civil rights groups. Many events followed the bridge worship service in the subsequent ten days. Church members or active groups were also responsible for these events. Once we also succeeded in inviting Walter Jens[2] and his wife[3] to give presentations, or Professor Bonhoeffer from the orga-

---

2. Walter Jens (1923–2013) was a German writer, philologist, literary historian, literary critic, and professor who taught most of his career at the Eberhard Karls University in Tübingen. While he received numerous honors for his work, he was also criticized for being a member of the National Socialist Party as a young adult. In response, he explained that he was enrolled in the party membership automatically because of his participation in the Hitler Youth.

3. Inge Jens (b. 1927) is a German linguist and pedagogue who gained particular recognition as an editor of literary works, including those of Thomas Mann (1875–1955). She also published several of her own books.

nization "Doctors against Nuclear Demise." The peace decade was always concluded in the evening of the day of repentance with a central ecumenical worship service in the Market Church or the St. Maurice Church. We did not limit our peace services to the peace decade. During the course of the year there were "services of lament," "Fasting for Peace" (twenty-four hours in the Market Church), and Stations of the Cross walks on various occasions, not only during Lent.

1983

Citizen Rights Groups in the Church

As "CHURCH FOR OTHERS" we had to be receptive to everything that concerned, troubled, and prompted human beings in our country to act. People who were socially at risk (released prisoners, alcoholics, among others), but also pacifists, for whom the establishment of construction soldiers units did not suffice, gathered together in the "Public Youth Work" organization. The pacifists wanted to perform "societal peace service" outside the military. Small groups also formed who deliberated about an "improved" or "democratic" socialism and also devised plans for it. Since the party had its informers everywhere, it learned about this. There were constant conflicts with the governmental authorities. In order to prevent this, conspiratorial operational methods were attempted. Could we justify this in the church? Was it not our mission to name injustice openly and without timidity, to demand democratic elections, and to request the publication of test data regarding air and water? And much more! There were also arrests, convictions, and deportations to the Federal Republic of Germany in Halle.

While the conflicts with the "Public Youth Work" escalated more and more, new groups with societal questions searched for contact with and support from us. We established three working groups of the ecclesiastical circuit:

- "The Ecological Work Group"
- "Christian Women for Peace"
- "Christian Physicians in Social Responsibility"

On the basis of what we learned from the conflicts related to "Public Work," competencies were agreed upon between the leadership of the groups and the leadership of the ecclesiastical circuit and spokespersons were designated who kept contact with us. Those of us from the church circuit leadership had learned to believe that the groups were capable of greater maturity. The responsible persons in the groups were mature and strong enough to accept responsibility for conflicts when difficulties arose. However, ultimate responsibility remained with the leadership of the ecclesiastical circuit. I do not want to conceal that the civil rights groups under the umbrella of the church were not universally approved, also within the church. Is this still ecclesiastical service? Do they not bring much agitation into our congregations?

Personally, I was thankful to the provost, Dr. Falcke from Erfurt, that he again and again supported our work with the working groups, both within the church and also with regard to the representatives of the government. In 1985 he presented a report in Halle to the Halle Missionary Conference that received much attention. He encouraged us to continue to work with the groups: "The groups have the sensory function in the church. The competence of the affected persons, who suffer because of the lack of peace in our world, is collected in the groups. The suffering are those who are first seized by the rising water of the flood while the others still sit on dry land. Whoever desires to do something to master the flood, whoever wishes to do something for the shalom future of the world, must listen carefully to those already afflicted, on whom the reports of the water level of the flood are to be read."

At this time the "applicants" who wanted to leave for the Federal Republic of Germany also increasingly came to us. They no longer had hope that something could still change in our country. It was particularly alarming when pastoral colleagues also made their application for departure from the country. I had to process such a disappointment twice in the St. Paul congregation. When even the pastors do not have hope anymore, why should members of the congregation still accept unfair treatments because of their loyalty to the congregation? I examined Pastor Hamel's encouraging book *Christ in the German Democratic Republic*[1] in home circles and groups.

---

1. Hamel, *Christ in der DDR*.

1984

Unexpected Consequences

I WROTE THE FOLLOWING letter to the mayor of Halle on August 4, 1984:

> Very honorable Sir Mayor!
>
> We were invited to a festive event by Mr. Hanke that is scheduled on August 29 in the concert hall on the occasion of the thirty-fifth anniversary of the German Democratic Republic. The trusting relationship between Christians and Marxists in our society is supposed to be expressed in this event.
>
> The leadership group of our church circuit has authorized me to write to you why we hesitate at this moment to accept this invitation.
>
> A few days ago I was summoned to appear before the district attorney of Halle as chairperson of the circuit church council and questioned about the content of a worship service of lament. In our view, this summons is a sign that our ecclesiastical work is viewed with great mistrust and judged to be a very dangerous matter by the state authorities. We are kept under very careful surveillance by the State Security personnel during our worship services and events. There is constant intervention in our event planning (this was very excessive on June 3 during our church circuit event in Neukirchen). Speakers are forbidden to appear at congregational events (for example, on June 26 at the St. Paul parish hall). Arrangements with the regional theater are canceled at short notice. We had proposed the performance of "The Great Peace" on September 20 and wanted to sell tickets for it.
>
> These are only a few examples which have made it clear to us how intensely we are distrusted in Halle. What other citizens and

groups are granted as a matter of course is prohibited to Christians: for example, a joint visit to the theater. We are extremely hurt by this. We understand when problems that have presented themselves are addressed openly. Solutions are also found then. There are enough examples for this, also in Halle. We stand by what I wrote to you, highly honored Sir Mayor, on the occasion of your installation and what you also confirmed in your response. We are sincere about a trusting cooperation between Christians and Marxists in our country. We want to contribute to the well-being of this city. However, that is made immensely more difficult for us by actions such as I have described for you above. We support honesty and openness in our dealings with one another. This is why I am writing this letter to you.

Your Helmut Hartmann, Superintendent, greets you.

I unintentionally caused great alarm with this letter, all the way to the governmental circles in Berlin. It was the basis of many conversations on the regional and national level. A stay in Lucerne (Switzerland) with my wife, on which I had been sent, was obviously denied. The relationship between state and church in Halle had become ice-cold in the fall of 1984. We devoted much time to analyzing the conditions in Halle during a pastoral retreat in Hirschluch in October. We agreed that we should continually seek anew a modus vivendi for dealing with the governmental authorities without betraying our mission and surrendering our independence. We sensed this at the time, but we know it now from the State Security Service files: the State Security Service also monitored and evaluated everything in Hirschluch.

1985

The Service of Visitation

IN AN OLD VISITATION order from 1948 it said, "The service of visitation is the most noble mission of the leadership of the church, which has the duty to check on the sisters and brothers, how they are." (See Acts 15:36.) Visitation of the congregations had already been practiced in this sense in Halle for some years. I continued this practice during my eight years as superintendent. During that time we visited nine of the twenty-eight congregations in our church circuit, among them four congregations on the outskirts of the city, two congregations in the newly built areas, and three congregations in the old area of the central city. The visitation group that was in service at a particular time consisted of about ten people. Some were members of the circuit church council and others came from neighboring congregations. One visitation lasted about two to three weeks. Plans for the visit were prepared several weeks before, and the visit was evaluated several weeks later.

During a visitation the visitors and the visited wrestled together in order to discover anew the gospel in our time. We formed a learning community together. We wanted to discover what "Church on the way into the Diaspora" or "Church within Socialism" meant concretely in Halle during our time. We visitors did not know this any better than those who were visited. Theologians and non-theologians were together in this learning community. Together we hoped for direction in pressing situations, such as internal and external emigration of close friends, the Cold War, destruction of the environment, resignation in our congregations, and so on.

In addition to such time-consuming visitation weeks, we also carried out visitations in the congregations as members of the circuit church council. These shorter visitations were completed by two or three people and were done for a particular reason, or we invited representatives of the congregations to join the circuit church council. Our circuit synod, which met twice a year, contributed considerably to the goal that the congregations of a church circuit would coalesce into a spiritual community. We also encouraged the congregational councils of neighboring congregations to meet together in order to promote regional cooperation.

In the previous year we had carried out an ecumenical project on the city level under the motto "Excursion to the Neighbor." Evangelicals, Roman Catholics, Baptists, Methodists, and Adventists participated. We mutually visited worship services and events of other confessions and consequently evaluated such visits in groups.

The bishops of our territorial church also understood their leadership function at that time primarily as visitation service. Bishop Dr. Krusche visited consecutively the individual spheres of work of our church. For our Halle church circuit it was important that Bishop Dr. Krusche became acquainted with the "Open Work" movement in Halle-Neustadt through his visit. Then he was able to make the following judgment on the basis of his own experience when dealing with the state authorities: "We find unequivocally that this kind of youth work is a form of service that must be done for the sake of our love for Christ."

His successor in the bishop's office, Dr. Demke,[1] visited four church circuits every year. He stayed a week in a particular church circuit and lived there in the congregations, visited colleagues and congregational members, and also went to the smallest and most difficult congregations. He began his service of visitation in the isolated congregations in the prohibited area

---

1. Christoph Demke (b. 1935) earned a doctorate and taught New Testament studies at the Evangelical Seminary in Berlin. He served as secretary of the Theological Commission in the Office of Secretary of the Association of Evangelical Churches in the German Democratic Republic from 1975 until 1977 and then as director of the Association from 1981 until 1983. In the latter year he became bishop of the Evangelical Church of the Church Province Saxony and served until 1997. He opposed the reunification of the two Germanys because he was one of the East German citizens who envisioned their country as a socialist alternative to the Federal Republic of Germany. However, he also participated in the conversations in Loccum that resulted in the reunification of the Evangelical territorial churches in the former East and West Germany into the Evangelical Church in Germany (Evangelische Kirche in Deutschland, EKD) in 1991.

The Service of Visitation

of the border between Germany and Germany. He did not allow himself to be welcomed like an ecclesiastical prince. He went as a brother among brothers and sisters in order to live with them for a week.

1986

City Mission Pastor, Erfurt

IN THE SUMMER OF 1986, ten years after the self-immolation of Pastor Oskar Brüsewitz, retired Bishop Dr. Krusche posed this question in a church magazine article, which was forbidden by the government censorship: "Does it still trouble us or have we meanwhile learned to affirm that we are a church without value, without power, without any identifiable successes and that there is nothing greater and more significant than to be used by Him as messengers of His love and instruments of His peace?"

With this question I said good-bye to the congregations and colleagues in the Halle church circuit in October 1986.

With this question I began my service as circuit pastor for community service and city mission in Erfurt in October 1986. I affirmed this question with hesitation and discovered with great astonishment in the following years how often we were used as Christ's instruments.

Two days after my installation I participated in the city mission pastors' convention in Berlin and had to present a short paper there on the theme "The city mission from the perspective of congregations and the church circuit." I was asked to make this contribution half a year earlier. At that time I did not suspect yet that I would be active as a city mission pastor half a year later. I had agreed to participate in a dangerous game. I could be taken at my word in Erfurt concerning everything that I spoke about at the Berlin conference regarding the expectations of the city mission from the perspective of the Halle church circuit.

City Mission Pastor, Erfurt

I demanded cooperation between the congregations and the city mission in Berlin. Without active congregations in the vicinity, a city mission cannot do justice to its calling in the city. And congregations stop being living congregations when they hand over all responsibility for social challenges to the city mission. There must be particular institutions for diaconal work with qualified employees. However, the congregations remain obligated to know that they are jointly responsible for this ministry. It is the particular assignment of the city mission to seek out new challenges for the church and also to attempt new spheres of work in a pioneering manner. Risks are connected with this, and setbacks and difficulties must be taken into account. It is all the more important not to abandon the linkage with the congregations.

In the short All Saints Street in the old city of Erfurt various spheres of work of the church met in closest proximity. The "All Saints Association" formed spontaneously. The circuit youth director, Matthias Sengewald, who lived around the corner; the Deacon, Wolfgang Musigmann of the "Open Work"; the Roman Catholic theologian, Ernst Günter, who directed the ecumenical St. Christopher Daycare Center for people with mental disabilities; the student pastor, Johannes Staemmler, and I met every few weeks during the first year, exchanged views about everything that concerned us, and mutually informed each other. This association seemed superfluous after several months. New challenges led us to form new groups. We had Paul Oestreicher,[1] the Anglican theologian from Coventry, as our guest during the peace decade in November 1986, only a few weeks after our start in Erfurt. I already knew him from previous meetings in Halle and the Lutherstadt Eisleben. He wrote in our guest book: "It is a joy to be the first guest in this beautiful home. Our first guest in Coventry came from the German Democratic Republic. A beautiful exchange of human beings!"

---

1. Paul Oestreicher (b. 1931) was born in Germany, but his family had to leave the country because of the Jewish ancestry of his father. They emigrated to New Zealand, where Oestreicher spent his youth. He eventually moved to England and was ordained an Anglican priest. He was an advocate of women's ordination and of world peace. Although he criticized the Soviet Union and its policies, he was able to make seventy-seven pastoral visits to the German Democratic Republic. During the 1980s he was actively involved in the anti-apartheid movement as the Director of International Affairs of the British Council of Churches. His election as bishop of Wellington, New Zealand was not approved by the church authorities. Instead, he served as canon and director of the International Center for Reconciliation at Coventry Cathedral from 1985 until 1997. His pacifist convictions inspired him to join the Quakers in addition to his affiliation with the Anglican community.

1987

A City that Deals Justly

ON MAY 7, 1987 the work group "The city and the environment in which we live" opened an exhibition in the St. Michael Church for the reclamation of the St. Andrew district. The city had planned the construction of an expressway that was supposed to run through the St. Andrew district, along the cathedral square, around the cathedral, and then connect to a beltway. The exhibition was prepared by experts from the construction industry and from the field of monument preservation under the theme "A justifiable traffic pattern in the city—a city that deals justly." Many courageous young people participated.

The exhibition immediately received the greatest attention, far beyond Thuringia. It was visited by about twelve thousand interested people in the following weeks.

The city council reacted immediately during the first days with prohibitions and threats against those responsible for the exhibition. On May 16 Senior Lauszat[1] and I were summoned to the city hall. We did not allow ourselves to be intimidated. We emphasized that with this exhibition we wanted to stimulate an open discussion regarding questions of urban development that interest the whole population. The more the exhibition was

---

1. The title "Senior" was given to the head of the ministerium in a particular city. This person was chosen for this leadership role by fellow pastors in the community. Hartmann's reference is to Pastor Hellmuth Lauszat (b. 1934), who served as senior in Erfurt from 1972 until 1996. During that time he represented the church in negotiations and conflicts with governmental authorities; was an advocate of democratic ideals; and promoted the toleration of diverse opinions, within both the church and the society.

discussed in official circles and among the population, the more visitors we were able to register.

The visitors recorded their opinion candidly and courageously in the displayed guest books. They also did not allow themselves to be deterred when it became known that one guest book after another disappeared and was analyzed in the Ministry of State Security.

On our part, we presented to the city council an evaluation of the exhibition in the form of a document of fourteen pages. It was only after we turned to the chairperson of the state council that we were received in the city hall for a discussion. However, we found no understanding. The responsible persons of the city boasted of their positions of power, questioned any competence regarding the matter on our part, and threatened us with severe consequences if we continued to remain active in this area. The group remained active until the political Wende in the fall of 1989.

The "Open Work" movement sharpened the protest against the planned construction projects a few months after the first exhibition with a second one under the theme "A city at the crossroads."

With the two exhibitions in the St. Michael Church we unexpectedly won many new friends and sympathizers who more or less openly acknowledged their support of our concerns: for example, from those interested in the preservation of monuments, from the interest group "Old University," from the working group "Cellar Research" of the Cultural Association, and from the Christian Democratic Union group "Central City" (in contrast to the Christian Democratic Union associations on the city and district level).

The demolition of old buildings in the St. Andrew district was stopped through all of these activities, at least slowed. We interpreted it to be signs of hope for the old city districts St. Andrew and St. Michael, which were threatened with demolition and disrepair, that the two church towers of St. George and St. Michael received new roofs in the fall of 1988 and the spring of 1989.

1988

Remain and Resist

I HAD USED THE theme "Remain in the country and resist daily!" to invite people to one of the weekday worship services after Easter. This is how I interpreted the Psalm verse: "Remain in the country and nourish yourself honestly."[1] (Ps 37:3) In this worship service on Wednesday at 5 p.m., I wanted to motivate the people with the subsequent homily to champion more justice and humaneness in our country. To my astonishment more and more young adults, who had made applications for emigration to the Federal Republic of Germany and were subject to diverse harassment and discrimination, came to these worship services week after week. Some had already waited six years for their departure from the country. After a few weeks the number of worship service attendees grew to an average of 150.

I related to the new challenges, provided opportunity for open discussions in connection with the worship services, and declared myself willing to have individual pastoral conversations. In doing so, I left no doubt that I considered it to be advisable to remain in the German Democratic Republic and to assist here so that something might change in the society. I encouraged this in every worship service. Of course, these worship services soon came to the attention of the State Security Service. On August 1, 1988 the action "Strategic Process Community"[2] was begun and carried on un-

---

1. This is the translation of the verse as quoted by Hartmann from Martin Luther's translation of Scripture. The New Revised Standard Version reads: "Trust in the Lord, and do good; so you will live in the land, and enjoy security." (Ps 37:3 NRSV)

2. The original reads Operativer Vorgang Gemeinde. The Operativer Vorgang was an intentional, undercover effort by the Ministry of State Security to identify and deal

til October 1989. The initiation of a "Strategic Inspection of Persons in the Community"[3] preceded it on June 9, 1988. Strategic consultations of the officers of the Ministry for State Security; ideas for planned conversations; and protocols and tape recordings from fourteen different informers, as well as their evaluations by the commanding officers of the security forces, are recorded in two volumes of about five hundred pages. The increasing nervousness of the governmental authorities is reflected in all of this. The State Security Service recorded precisely during the Wednesday worship service before the Erfurt church conference, which was held from June 10 to 12, 1988, what the worship attendees knew about the occupation of the cathedral by people who had made application to leave the country and how the worshippers reacted to the occupation. Through inquiries I was informed that the twenty-one people who participated in the occupation of the cathedral had left the church again on June 8 so that the cathedral could be used for events related to the church conference. Six weeks later, on July 21, 1988, a married couple began a hunger strike in our St. Michael Church after the Wednesday worship service in order to force their departure from the country. I supplied the couple with blankets and tea and locked them into the church with the urgent plea that they reconsider their decision. Since the couple persisted in their plan, the next morning I informed the Division of Internal Affairs of the city council at the request of the couple and organized a conversation with the applicants in the city hall, with the condition that the city council guaranteed that there would be no arrest. I informed the city council that I would wait in front of the city hall until the young people came out again. That happened an hour later. They were assured that they would receive the papers permitting departure from the country within three months. This promise was kept. I do not know whether they had to make any commitment in return.

The State Security Service analyzed very carefully how such days as May 1, May 8, August 6, August 13, September 1, October 7, or December 10 (human rights day) were reflected in our worship services and how we commented on such events as the local elections on May 7, 1989 or the bloody events on the Tiananmen Square in Beijing in July 1989.

---

with all opponents of the state. The strategic processes were often focused on specific groups or individuals.

3. The original reads Operative Personenkontrolle Gemeinde.

1989

The Miracle

THE NEWSLETTER OF THE Evangelical City Mission Erfurt of January 1989 expresses with what hopes but also with what fears we began the year 1989:

> The yearning of human beings for more freedom and happiness and human rights increased and the readiness for responsible communal participation and thinking increased during the time when Mikhail Gorbachev ruled in Moscow and attempted a new political way and when other politicians shied away in the face of the consequences of the new thinking and looked to Moscow warily. On the other hand, hatred and retaliation also hardened the hearts of people and legitimate nationalistic concerns turned into disastrous and dangerous chauvinism.
>
> At the same time the earth shook and fifty thousand people died under the rubble in the villages and cities of Armenia and many more women, children, and senior citizens had to be evacuated. Airplanes fell from the sky into densely populated towns and burned hundreds of people.
>
> In this time Jesus was newly discovered as the little brother of the weeping and fleeing and freezing, as the incarnate God, as the true human being. Whoever experienced this as the Christmas miracle of 1988 may also continue to recount it in the new year. We Christians have nothing that is more necessary than that we encourage each other to do this!

Before Easter 1989 we endeavored to organize an art exhibit of Erfurt artists in our church. The artistic works were to be offered for sale. The profits of the sale were intended for support of the earthquake victims in Armenia. We invited the Soviet vice-consul from Leipzig to the opening of the exhibit on Easter Monday. He had promised his attendance. On Monday morning I had to cancel his invitation because Erfurt artists had been pressured by the city council and no longer dared to display their paintings in our church. On April 5 there was a severe dispute over these incidents with the woman mayor during a conversation in the city hall.

We had had greater success in February of this year. The "Revolutionary Youth Organization Campuchia" had rented our Johannes Lang House[1] for a long weekend. Young people from Campuchia, who studied in the German Democratic Republic or completed a skilled labor apprenticeship, met in order to discuss their situation after all of the political movements that had begun in Asia and Eastern Europe. We had learned from the embassy in Berlin that this youth organization experienced greater and greater difficulties in the German Democratic Republic. The young people stayed overnight with Erfurt families. With gratitude they invited their hosts to an evening meal in the large assembly hall during which the young people demonstrated an aspect of their culture with songs and dances. They were also very interested to learn something about our churches and our societal conditions.

Through such large events, foreigners from Eastern Europe also became aware of us: namely, Poles, Lithuanians, Ukrainians, and Russians. In 1988 and 1989 my wife and I were guests of Lithuanian families in Druskininkai and Vilnius. We traveled throughout Lithuania, as far as Kleipeda (Memel). We visited the bishop of the small Lutheran Church in Lithuania in Taurage and experienced the initial, hesitant attempts at an independence movement. We participated in a mass demonstration in Vilnius. Police and demonstrators stood opposing each other for an hour in silence and without violence!

We visited the old Trakai fortress, whose historical significance as the first capital of Lithuania was newly recollected. As Lithuanians who lived in Erfurt learned about our travels to Lithuania, they requested that we show an exhibition about the independence movement in their country in our church. We made this possible. The summer of 1989 was an exciting one!

Our disappointing experiences during the attempt to denounce openly the proven election irregularities during the local elections of May

---

1. The Johannes-Lang-Haus is the community center of the Evangelical City Mission in Erfurt. It hosts various events, including seminars, cultural programs, and special celebrations.

7 and the news reports of the bloody events on Tiananmen Square in Beijing spread resignation and weariness among our civil rights groups. A courageous decision of the circuit church council in September to open all churches and parish halls immediately to the new political movements (for example, New Forum, Democratic Emergence, Social Democratic Party of Germany, and so on) again awakened new hopes.

We had already encountered the greatest mistrust on the part of the governmental authorities in the spring, during our preparations for the day of St. Martin on November 10, because of the theme "Christ tears down the fences between the nations" (Eph 2:14). This theme expressed our concern about the expatriates in our country and about our eastern neighbors in Poland and Czechoslovakia. The governmental authorities on the city and district level feared that the expected forty thousand participants on St. Martin's Day might call out in choruses of voices: "The Berlin Wall has to go!" In August we stopped all negotiations with the governmental authorities and did without the permission to print materials. However, we declared that we would retain the theme in the way that we understood it. We looked forward to November 10 with anticipation and also with fears.

It was certainly moving when on November 10, one day after the opening of the wall, an event that is still not conceivable, I could greet the many thousand children and adults on the Cathedral Square with the biblical word: "Christ tears down the fences between the nations."

1990

A Hope Learns to Walk

THE FOLLOWING QUOTATION IS from a speech that I gave on October 24, 1990 in the baroque assembly hall of the Old Residence in Erfurt:

> A hope learned to walk in the last years. I walked with it, together with others. Many small steps were necessary before it became the way of hundreds of thousands in the fall of 1989. As I began my work in Erfurt four years ago, I already met tireless bearers of hope who did not allow themselves to be discouraged, even by disappointments. For example, among them belonged the few Evangelical and Roman Catholic women who held their peace prayer in the St. Lawrence Church week after week for eleven years. Their prayer evolved into the prayers of thousands of human beings in the fall of 1989.
>
> A hope learned to walk, in Leipzig, in Dresden, in Halle, in Erfurt, and elsewhere. We could participate in it and experience it as well. The willingness to dialogue in situations in which such dialogue barely still seemed to be appropriate was also part of this hope. It was a difficult learning process to bring people who thought differently and believed differently, atheists, secularized people, and people with different political opinions, into dialogue with one another. We argued, discussed, and sometimes questioned each other's good will. On our way, we were torn this way and that way, between resignation and hope. It was often a narrow way between accommodation and rebellion. There were passionate arguments between grass-roots groups and official ecclesiastical bodies. Blessed be those congregations and church circuits and

synods that took a deep breath and did not stop the dialogue. In this we mutually retained a sensitivity toward threatened people and an openness to the pending political problems.

As long as I have been active in the pastoral office—since 1958—the conversations with those who had political power were difficult and contentious. At the beginning we still met old communists at times who had suffered much during the Nazi period. They had retained an understanding for those who thought differently. However, more and more we met officials who only wanted to demonstrate their political power toward us. We attempted to discover, also in them, human beings with some independence in their thinking and feeling.

We were either summoned to the city hall and had to answer for events, worship services, exhibitions, or for some statements; or we requested conversations because events troubled us or because threatened people had asked us to intercede for them. There were horrible encounters during which an ice-cold atmosphere ruled. I am thinking of the conversations after the local elections in Erfurt in May 1989 or of the meetings before and after the worship services on October 7. Those were not dialogues. Severe censures were dispensed and strong threats were made. However, there were also topical discussions that resulted in progress regarding a particular matter. And sometimes there were also amazingly open and honest dialogues, most of the time only in one-on-one settings.

It was a highly contested question how far our willingness to dialogue could go. Conversations were, of course, also misused and repeated publicly with distortion. The willingness to have conversations could be interpreted as weakness. A status mentality caused us to hesitate. Might it harm the respect of the church if we hold conversations with unpopular representatives of the government and party? I always objected to this. As long as there is still a chance to be listened to in a dialogue one should continue to have conversations. And as long as there is mutual conversation, no force is employed. When we were invited to open dialogue in the city hall on October 24 last year, everything was actually already too late. Nevertheless, we went there. Most of you were witnesses to how it proceeded. The old city government as well as the party leadership were no longer able to have a conversation.

The conversations at the round tables that occurred at various levels in the following weeks as well as the conversations and discussions in the citizens committee were hopeful attempts at responsible deliberations regarding difficult problems. If we could only keep some of this alive in our parliamentary democracy!

The poet and pastor Albrecht Goes[1] once wrote:

"Whoever believes does not flee from his joint responsibility for the decisions of the day because of a joint concern for peace in the world. As far as I am concerned, I would rather lose face again and again with a willingness to negotiate than to suffocate in an ironclad certainty. I would rather allow myself to be disappointed once and more than once than that I deliberately slam a door that Christ did not slam."[2]

This is how I would like my activities related to the Wende to be understood. Our church should also perceive its responsibility in the building of new social relationships in the united Germany in this manner.

---

1. Albrecht Goes (1908–2000) served as a parish pastor from 1930 until he was drafted and worked as a radio operator in Romania. He was also a hospital chaplain during the war years. After World War II he returned to parish ministry until 1953. He then devoted himself to his vocation as a writer, although he also continued to preach in churches regularly. Goes was a successful writer, publishing both poetry and prose works, and was inducted into the Berlin Academy of the Arts. He addressed the Holocaust and sought to foster Jewish-Christian dialogue and reconciliation through his literary work, particularly the novel *The Burnt Offering*. He was also a peace proponent and opposed German rearmament.

2. The translation is of the quotation as it appears in the memoir.

1991

Day of Unity[1]

OCTOBER 3, 1 P.M.: There is colorful activity everywhere in the city, similar to a fair, with music and booths. Families stroll from one festival area to another in beautiful weather. It is a peaceful picture. There are some posters on the walls of houses: "Invitation to prayer for peace in our city." Is the peaceful picture only an illusion?

3 p.m.: The Dominican Church is filling up for an ecumenical worship service. On Monday evening representatives of churches, parties and groups, Christians and non-Christians, had met with the mayor on short notice in the city hall. It was decided that there should be a public event in the Dominican Church in order to demonstrate convincingly solidarity with the expatriate fellow residents in our city. An event of the National Democratic Party[2] was scheduled in the afternoon at the same time but was canceled at short notice on the same day.

After addresses by Provost Dr. Falcke and Bishop Dr. Wanke[3] in the worship service, a group of young people suddenly appeared and unrolled

---

1. From an article for a church periodical.

2. The National Democratic Party is a political party in Germany with a xenophobic, nationalistic agenda.

3. Joachim Wanke (b. 1941) is a Roman Catholic priest who served as professor of New Testament Exegesis in the Erfurt seminary, where he had also studied. He was ordained a bishop in 1980 and appointed apostolic administrator of the episcopal office of the Diocese Erfurt-Meiningen in 1981 and as bishop of the newly formed Erfurt Diocese in 1994. During his episcopal ministry he served as chairperson of the commission that produced a new German translation of Scripture and was eager to facilitate the

a poster with the words of Martin Niemoeller: "We were silent when the communists, the Social Democrats, and the Jews were sent to the concentration camps. When we were arrested, there was no one left who could have cried out for us!"[4]

The young people challenged the visitors of the worship service to walk a "Martin Niemoeller path" against the Nazis and on behalf of the expatriates.

They went into the street alone. We continued our worship service with the intercession for peace in our city accompanied by the concern about what could now very well happen on the street. At the conclusion of the worship service it was announced that a demonstration in opposition to the hostility against expatriates is scheduled to take place the following Thursday in connection with the peace prayer at the St. Lawrence Church.

5:30 p.m.: Six young people, approximately fourteen years old, appear in front of the Johannes Lang House with clubs in their hands. They are looking for the "house with the Vietnamese." I call attention to the fact that a private meeting is occurring on the theme "Should the Vietnamese remain in the country or return to Viet Nam?" The young people are not satisfied. They want to participate in the meeting. I respond: "However, only without the clubs!" The young people: "However, we need the clubs as protection against the fascists!" Only now do I understand. The young people want to protect the expatriates against attacks. I attempt to make it clear to them that the use of force does not bring peace into our city. I remind them of the peaceful revolution a year ago. The young people react as if they had never heard something about peace prayers and demonstrations. They marched on with their clubs like children who play war and do not know how horrible wars are.

8 p.m.: A public Vietnamese evening has begun in the Johannes Lang House with many German guests. They celebrate peacefully and cheerfully.

10 p.m.: The police prevent an attack on a home for asylum seekers.

---

proclamation of the gospel in a secularized country.

4. Various versions of this statement have circulated since the 1940s. Niemoeller himself offered various wordings during his lifetime.

1992

In Polish East Prussia

A MUTUAL ENGAGEMENT CONFERENCE of the Evangelical Churches of Hessen-Nassau and the Church Province Saxony and of the Lutheran Church of Poland brought us together in Mikołajki (Masuria) in May 1992. We mutually introduced ourselves in short reports about our spheres of work, our hopes, and our disappointments. There were interesting discussions, and we learned many new things about the history and the contemporary situation of the Polish Evangelical Church.

A few months later, in August, Christiane and I traveled privately throughout Poland. We began in Warsaw, which was completely destroyed by the Germans during the war. The Poles were no longer supposed to have a political and cultural center. However, the Poles rebuilt their capital city again after the war under the most difficult circumstances and with much love and great respect for the architecture of their ancestors. We walked quietly and dismayed through the city districts where indescribable scenes played out during the Warsaw uprisings. We stopped at the monument where Willy Brandt knelt. With this genuflection he ushered in the Eastern policy of the German Federal Republic against the vehement opposition of the conservative powers. We stayed several days in Mikołajki and discovered for ourselves the beautiful, quiet Masuria by foot, by train, or by bus. We thought often about Siegfried Lenz,[1] the writer who was born

---

1. Siegfried Lenz (1926–2014) was a German writer who published numerous novels, short stories, and plays. He was a member of the Social Democratic Party and supported the Eastern Policy of Willy Brandt. He had himself been born in East Prussia, which is now Poland. In his writings, he sought to confront Germany's recent history and

and grew up in Masuria and about his books, for example, *So zärtlich war Sulejken* or *The German Lesson*. We learned to love the quiet lakes and reverently passed by a secluded Orthodox cloister where three old nuns supposedly still live. We were delighted that old village churches had been renovated carefully with a colorful rustic baroque décor. We inspected Olsztyn (Allenstein). Masuria was ruled from here. We were impressed by the medieval Malbork Castle, a fortress of the Teutonic Order. Hitler's Wolf's Lair, where an assassination attempt on Hitler was made on July 20, 1944, made a somber impression on us.

On the Polish shore of the Baltic Sea we were reminded of turbulent times of the old history. The Hanseatic city, Gdansk, has been marvelously rebuilt again. We found a friendly night's lodging in a house located directly on the shipyard. The hostess could tell us much about Wałęsa[2] and his striking shipyard workers. Old artillery in Sopot and Gdynia reminded people of World War II. We experienced an organ concert in a rebuilt church in Elbląg. The rebuilding of the whole old city was being prepared. We drove from Elbląg to Frombork (Frauenburg). The uncle of Copernicus once resided in the fortress-like bishop's palace. He granted the security and freedom to his famous nephew to pursue his scientific studies of the universe. We could not travel to the Vistula Spit, which lies opposite Frombork, because of high waves and dense fog. We looked longingly over the Baltic Sea. We remembered an old song about the elks on the Baltic. In the song it says at the conclusion, "They again go away slowly, animals of a time long ago. And they disappear in the distant fog, as in the large gate of eternity . . ." In the meantime disturbing news reached us from Germany. Neo-Nazis apparently had gone on a rampage against expatriates for five days and nights in Rostock-Lichtenhagen.

---

to promote the quest for peace.

2. Lech Wałęsa (b. 1943) is the founder of Solidarity, the first independent labor union formed in the Soviet Bloc countries. He became a labor activist as an electrician in the Lenin shipyards of Gdansk and was persecuted by the Soviets for his activities. However, his fellow workers supported his efforts. Those efforts also had crucial political implications for and contributed to the eventual dissolution of the Soviet Union. Wałęsa was awarded the Nobel Peace Prize in 1983 and served as Poland's president from 1990 to 1995.

1993

Melting Heart

MEDITATION ON PSALM 22—AFTER A HEART OPERATION

Wonderfully rescued by capable powers..."
Where is this certainty after the heart operation
in the horrible condition between anesthetization and wakefulness?
When the mind is not operating no prayer texts are at hand.
The familiar melodies of Taizé are distant.

I am experiencing what the person praying Psalm 22 did.
(I only became aware of this later!)
My heart melts like wax. I am dissolving. Is this dying?
I discover myself bound by my hands. There are tubes everywhere, straps,
connected with fittings. They press me down,
tie me to the bed. My tongue sticks to my gum;
my throat is dry like a potsherd.
I am watched from the front and from the back.
I am not allowed to drink; my quota is already met.
Nightmares startle me.
Women nurses, angels a moment ago, become dangerous demons.
Calming and encouraging words from doctors and caregivers
are pushed into the background by cries, laughter, threats
experienced in such a way in nightmares.

Melting Heart

God, you are so far away! Why have you forsaken me?
I am so exhausted, without hope. I am poured out like water.
My organs dissolve.
God, you are so far away! And I had believed:
"Wonderfully rescued by capable powers..."

Suddenly, there is a groaning in the intensive care unit.
It is not coming from me.
Another human being suffers with me in the same room.
I cannot see him.
I have no strength to speak with him.
I loudly speak my first name in the eerie room: Helmut.
And I receive a response: Gottfried.
(A miner from Zwickau, as I learn later.)
The spell was broken. Another person suffers with me.
He is also bound, tied to the bed.
He has thirst as I do and is frightened by nightmares.
Is the night not going to end?
It ends. You have heard me, Gottfried!
And with Gottfried, Jesus of Nazareth.
He cries out with me on the cross of Golgatha:
"My God, my God, why have you forsaken me?"
And this cry is heard.
God's absence transforms itself into God's nearness.
You have heard me.

Two days after the operation during a wide-awake moment,
two of my adult children are close to my bed.
Through the window there is a wide view of snowy woods
in the blinding sunlight.
Easter joy fills me before the night spreads out once again.
You have answered me, God! My heart shall revive,
my repaired heart.
I will tell my children and grandchildren
how God's absence has transformed itself into God's nearness.

In the congregation in Bad Berka

The Quest for Faithfulness

God's presence shall be confirmed ever anew.
The patients in the hospitals,
the doctors, women nurses, and caregivers in Bad Berka
are dependent on this.
When individuals cry out in the night:
"Why are you so far away, God?";
when doctors and women nurses work diligently
with passion and golden fingers,
to repair sick hearts,
the local congregation believes and bears witness
in devotions, worship services, at the Eucharistic table:
"Wonderfully rescued by capable powers
we await confidently whatever may come.
God is with us in the evening and in the morning,
and certainly every new day!"

1994

To Jesus's Table

As a consequence of our public ecclesiastical work in Halle and in Erfurt a picture of the church crowded into my mind. The church is like a tent with a wide roof, but with open walls all the way around. Everyone who wishes can enter from all sides. Everyone is invited without prerequisites. Neither a baptismal certificate, nor a church tax notification, nor a police certificate of good conduct is requested, nor are there inquiries about national origin or social circumstances.

Jesus's table stands under this roof, visible to all. All who wish to come find a place at this table. Everyone is invited, but no one is compelled.

Those who are responsible for such a wide-open church keep close contact with this table. Otherwise, they would not persist with this openness.

Jesus's table in the church has something to do with the tables in the "Restaurant of the Heart,"[1] or in the soup kitchen; and also with the tables in prison cells, in the women's shelter, or in a homeless shelter; also with the stones under the Krämerbrücke[2] that are used as tables by the homeless and street children.

---

1. The "Restaurant of the Heart" serves people in need in Erfurt during the winter months of December and January. Its expenses are covered chiefly by donations, but guests are also expected to pay one euro for a main meal, coffee, and dessert. Volunteers staff the restaurant. There is also a "Restaurant of the Heart" in Leipzig. The Restaurant of the Heart movement was initiated by the French comedian and actor Coluche (Michel Colucci 1944–1986).

2. The Krämerbrücke is a merchants' bridge in the central city of Erfurt with stores on the ground floor of the buildings constructed on the bridge and homes on the upper floors.

Out of consideration for alcoholics we have replaced wine with grape juice during the meal celebrations in the worship services. When homeless people with skin diseases happened to come to our worship services, we replaced the grape juice with grapes. No one should feel excluded, neither the sick nor the healthy who no longer wanted to participate in the meal celebrations because of fear of contagion.

In the church, a festively set table to which everyone has access can pass on the message of Jesus's invitation to all more effectively than scriptural readings or sermons. We left it open whether our meal celebrations were understood as celebrations of the Lord's Supper or as love meals (agape meals). All share that Jesus is the one who invites. We wanted to make this, and nothing else, clear.

An unknown homeless man came into the breakfast room of the staff members on a Friday during a ministry meeting, sat down matter-of-factly among them, and shared in the breakfast. I sensed that annoyance and indignation were welling up among the staff members. Can we not be alone by ourselves once during the week without the people who pester us and constantly expect too much of us? I started the meal before this sentiment erupted. I requested that the guest be provided with everything necessary. After the meal the stranger arose and left us just as he had come, quietly and without a word to anyone. The night before we had begun the night of the homeless in Erfurt. Some of the staff members had spent the night with homeless people in the Anger.[3] All of our solidarity with the homeless that we wanted to confirm with this activity would have become inauthentic if we had dismissed the stranger from our sumptuously set breakfast table the next morning. In 1994 unusual announcements appeared in the *Thüringer Allgemeinen* during the course of the year:

> "Take care that you do not despise one of these little ones,"
> (Mat 18:10 NRSV) says Jesus.
>
> N. N. born on . . ., died on the street.
> Funeral at the St. Michael Church.
> The Evangelical City Mission extends the invitation.

We wanted to alert the public about people who live, suffer, and die next to us anonymously. Because they also belong to those invited by Jesus, we name their names publicly. Germans and foreigners were among them.

---

3. The Anger is the center of the city of Erfurt. It is now the main business and shopping district.

1995

A Christmas Story

IT HAPPENED DURING OUR time that the law of the market economy determined everything, and the only thing that was asked was what profit can be expected. A selfish and competitive mindset poisoned the communal life of people. Those who had much became ever more wealthy, and those who had nothing became ever poorer.

A strange picture presented itself under one of the arches of the Krämerbrücke on Christmas Eve—the streets were empty; warm candlelight shone from the Christmas rooms. Joseph from Nigeria and Mary from Erfurt sat huddled together closely. Mary held a little boy with a dark complexion and bright eyes in her arms. Some street children, who begged during the day on the Wenigemarkt,[1] had placed themselves protectively around the parental couple with the child. In their hands, numbed by the cold, they carried empty beer cans into which they had inserted candles. Very near them a tributary of the Gera River flowed passed them on which some ducks sleepily allowed themselves to be carried back and forth.

At the same time, fifteen-year-old Mario and seventeen-year-old Jörg sat in the remand prison on the cathedral plaza. They attempted to help each other so that the Christmas rage did not gain power over them. They had heard that in the previous year a despairing Christmas mood had driven young people to carry out a prison revolt.

---

1. The Wenigemarkt is a small marketplace in the central city of Erfurt and is located in the near vicinity of the Krämerbrücke.

A star could be seen on a small Christmas banner that they had placed on their table. "The Christmas star?" Mario asked smiling and skeptically. Jörg gestured sadly in the negative: "Not for us." Then they heard steps in the hallway. The door was unlocked. The social worker looked in on them one more time. "I am going home now," said Mr. Littmann. "Many thanks that you stopped by to see us one more time!" Jörg called out bravely. "And greet the Christmas star from us. It must certainly shine somewhere on Christmas Eve!" Mario added bitterly.

After Mr. Littmann had unlocked and locked six iron doors, he stood outside on the street that led to the cathedral square. It was quiet today where yesterday a colorful hustle and bustle of the Christmas market still prevailed. Only the festive fir tree all lit up still stood majestically on the large, wide square. The beautiful crèche with the carved figures—Mary and Joseph, the child, ox and donkey, the shepherds, the kings—had disappeared. It was supposedly set up in the cathedral so that many church attendees could delight in it during the Christmas days. Mr. Littmann walked across the large cathedral square. He saw many stars in the clear sky. "Greet the Christmas star from us!" Mr. Littmann remembered that this is what the young prisoners had called to him. He could not recognize a Christmas star in the sky. The starry sky was far away, inaccessible, cold.

Mr. Littmann passed many brightly lighted shop windows on Market Street. They were alive with sparkling stars, large ones and small ones. However, he could not discover the Christmas star.

The road led him further over the Fischmarkt,[2] past the Krämerbrücke. There he noticed a weak gleam of light under the left arch of the bridge. He had almost missed it. He stepped closer. Then he saw several people, closely huddled together, as if they wanted to warm each other. And then he discovered the little child. He could not fathom it. On Christmas Eve, when it was so cold, a small child under the Krämerbrücke! And those who stood around the parents and child like angels, with candles in beer cans, they were also still children, perhaps twelve or thirteen years old. Who knew what would become of them one day. Perhaps in two years they would also sit under interrogation arrest on the cathedral square like Mario and Jörg today. Then the children's song "From heaven above to earth I come . . ." sounded from a small harmonica. Mr. Littmann knew the musician. Willy had no home but also did not want to enter the homeless shelter

---

2. The Fischmarkt is another marketplace in the center of Erfurt, where the city hall is located.

in Mittelhäuser Street. He had become afraid of people. He had cirrhosis of the liver and lived somewhere on the street. He always had his harmonica with him. He was now playing the well-known Christmas song under the Krämerbrücke. No one sang along, but all were listening. Behind the musician, Mr. Littmann discovered a married couple. They also belonged to the Erfurt street scene. They were both alcoholics and made their life very difficult. Now they stood very quietly, hand in hand, and looked at the child.

And then more and more came from the soup kitchen, from the "Restaurant of the Heart," from the homeless shelter, from the women's shelter, from the groups of all of the welfare organizations, from the home of the asylum seekers. Mr. Littmann recognized Mustafa and Sophia from Bosnia and Ali with his friends from Mauritania. The one arch of the Krämerbrücke was no longer sufficient. All of the arches of the bridge, the area at the water's edge, the bridge above, and the entrances from all sides were filled. Those who had lost so much, who were threatened so dangerously, who had to live in the dark shadow of society were all standing close together.

Suddenly it appeared to Mr. Littmann that the candles of the street children were becoming brighter and brighter. The whole vicinity of the Krämerbrücke now appeared in a radiant light. Was this not the Christmas star that he was supposed to greet from the two young prisoners? The many poor people looked expectantly at the small child of color on the lap of Mary.

And then a rejoicing began throughout the city of Erfurt. Initially it was only the oldest bell of the city from the year 1392, which hangs in the tower of the small St. Michael Church. Then the largest bell of Erfurt, the Gloriosa of the Cathedral, raised its powerful voice and all of the bells of the city joined in the Christmas jubilation:

> Glory to God in the highest and peace on earth.
> Christmas sings a new song:
> A garden for the children, a house for the homeless,
> work for the unemployed, freedom for the prisoners,
> a future for the young people, understanding for the senior citizens,
> a doctor for the sick, a homeland for the strangers,
> bread for the hungry, peace to those in war's distress,
> a light for all those in darkness!
> This is what the Christmas story proclaims.

Mr. Littmann came to his senses again. Did he just dream? Mr. Littmann stood all alone on the street. It was quiet and dark around him. Some figures moved in the dark under the Krämerbrücke. Apparently they were preparing their beds. One heard the quiet whimpering of the small child periodically. A small candle still flickered faintly on a dark stone. Suddenly Mr. Littmann knew that he had discovered the Christmas star. Tomorrow he intended to tell the young prisoners where he found it.

1996

The Compassionate Romanian[1]

JESUS SAID TO A man who wanted to follow Him: "You must love your God with your whole heart and your neighbor as yourself."[2] "Who, then, is my neighbor?" the man asks in response. Jesus answers with the story of a Jewish man who was attacked by thieves on his way from Jerusalem to Jericho and was rescued by a Samaritan. (See Luke 10:25–37.) I want to retell the story now, adapted to our country and our time, by sharing the story of the compassionate Romanian.

There was a Weissenfels businessman who was still traveling in his car in the evening. He was hailed at a lonely place near Rudelsburg. A hitchhiker wanted a ride. However, this was a trap. Suddenly a number of men surrounded the stopped car. They pulled the businessman onto the street, beat him severely, robbed him, and disappeared with his car. The seriously injured man remained lying helplessly on the side of the road.

Some time later a pastor came speeding past with his car. He was in a hurry. He was expected in Bad Kösen for a bible class. The questions suddenly passed through his mind: "Was there not a man lying on the side of the road? Or was that simply an illusion?" "It was certainly an illusion," he reassured himself. "Who would be lying on the road at this time of the evening?" Thus he traveled on and led his bible class in Bad Kösen.

A short time later a social worker drove past. He was supposed to give a lecture to a welfare organization in Naumburg. The same thing happened

---

1. For a worship service on Diakonia Day in Weissenfels
2. In the biblical story, recorded in Luke, Jesus does not say this to the lawyer who questioned him. Rather, the man says this in response to a question by Jesus.

to him that happened to the pastor. "Was there not someone lying on the side of the road?" However, the car had already passed. "It was likely nothing serious." Besides, he had to give a very important lecture.

Finally, a Romanian asylum seeker came riding his bicycle. Startled, he stopped. He almost drove over the seriously injured person. He bent over the man, put his jacket under his head, gave him a drink from his juice bottle, and considered what he should do. Then another car came. The headlights darted over the street. The Romanian jumped up and waved both arms excitedly. The car stopped. The Romanian told about the seriously injured man in broken German. A married couple got out of the car. They determined that medical help was urgently needed here. They carefully lifted the Weissenfels businessman onto the rear seat of the car and drove him directly to the Naumburg hospital.

"Who is my neighbor?" This was the question a man asked Jesus. The story provides a clear answer. The attacked man, who lay on the side of the road, was the neighbor of the pastor, the social worker, the Romanian, and the married couple. The Romanian and the married couple fulfilled Jesus's command: "Love your neighbor as yourself." Whoever desires to follow Jesus must act in the same way.

1997

Crooked Tree—Erect Walk

WHEN IT WAS DISCOVERED in 1994 that I had Parkinson's disease, I understood it to be a small, harmless addition to my heart disease. I wondered why acquaintances and friends reacted with much concern when I told them about this additional disease.

My six-week stay in the Parkinson clinic in Biskirchen near Wetzlar three years later enabled me to recognize how greatly I had underestimated the whole extent of Parkinson's disease until that time. I was still relatively well. However, I became quite disconcerted by the helplessness and misery and discouragement that I saw there.

The famous philosopher from Königsberg, Immanuel Kant,[1] described a senseless human life as a "crooked tree." Is a person sick with Parkinson's disease with his "shaking palsy," with his ankyloses, with his slow movements, with his overreactions, with his depressions, not similar to a "crooked tree" that is no longer useful for anything? A person sick with Parkinson's disease can no longer hope for recovery because the ultimate cause of his illness is still unknown today. The many very expensive medicines can control and reduce the effects of this illness, but they cannot heal it.

"I am utterly bowed down and prostrate; all day long I go around mourning," complains the person praying Psalm 38:6 (NRSV). A "crooked tree" is truly an appropriate picture for a person ill with Parkinson's disease.

1. Immanuel Kant (1724–1804) was one of the leading philosophers of the Enlightenment whose insights have shaped contemporary philosophical perspectives in profound ways. He was also an advocate of democratic institutions, which, he believed, would foster peace in the world.

The Quest for Faithfulness

In his book *Krummes Holz–aufrechter Gang,* the well-known theologian Helmut Gollwitzer[2] wants to make it clear that Kant's vision of the human being is only a half-truth. A human being can engage in an erect walk also as a "crooked tree." Gollwitzer experienced this during times of persecution, during war experiences, and during a long imprisonment. Erect walking is possible. It helps a person to cope with the situation of the crooked tree. The theologian borrows the phrase "erect walk" from the philosophical work of the socialist Ernst Bloch,[3] titled *The Principle of Hope.* In spite of terrible disappointments—as a socialist he had to give up his philosophy teaching position in Leipzig during the time of the German Democratic Republic—he does not abandon his hope for the erect walk of a human being. He draws his confidence from texts of the Old Testament and the New Testament. He guides the human and political hopes to more just, more peaceful, and healthier conditions on the basis of biblical salvation history. Also a human being who resembles the "crooked tree" can shape his life with energy and hope. "A hope learns to walk"—this is the way we mutually encouraged each other in ecclesiastical and citizen rights matters in the years before the Wende.

We also voice such mutual encouragements in the Dessau self-help group for those ill with Parkinson's disease. We meet every Wednesday in two groups of about forty-five women and men, some of whom are marked more and others less by the disease. We do physiotherapy with professional

---

2. Helmut Gollwitzer (1908–1993) was an Evangelical theologian who completed his doctorate at Basel with Karl Barth. He was a member of the Confessing Church and succeeded Martin Niemöller as pastor in Berlin-Dahlem after the arrest of Niemöller. While serving as a medic on the Eastern Front he was captured and was a Russian prisoner of war from 1945 until 1949. After his release he taught theology at the University of Bonn and the Free University of Berlin between 1950 and his retirement in 1975. Gollwitzer was a Christian Socialist, an advocate of peace and an opponent of nuclear proliferation, and a critic of capitalism.

3. Ernst Bloch (1885–1977) was a socialist philosopher who had to flee Germany because of his Jewish heritage. He wrote his *The Principle of Hope,* to which Hartmann refers, while residing in the United States. In 1948 he was invited to return to Germany and to assume a professorship at the University of Leipzig. During the subsequent years he became the leading political philosopher in the German Democratic Republic. However, the suppression of the Hungarian revolt caused him to become a critic of the Soviet Union and of the East German regime. He was, therefore, forced to retire in 1957. He subsequently left East Germany and settled in Tübingen where he was appointed to an honorary chair in philosophy. His utopian philosophical perspectives have influenced liberation theology and the theology of hope.

Crooked Tree—Erect Walk

instruction. We discuss our problems together and also celebrate together. The oldest woman is eighty years old. The youngest man is fifty years old.

"Crooked trees" are capable of an "erect walk," also when we do so while using crutches, or a wheelchair, or a hospital stay as assistance.

1998

The Three Informers of King Herod

AFTER TEN YEARS I was once again in a church. I had purchased the tickets for the Christmas Oratorio[1] in a bookstore. No one knew me there.

During a moment when particularly numerous attendees pressed through the church entrance I slipped in with them. I absolutely did not want to be recognized, for it was in this church that I often engaged in observations and made reports about them at the directions of the State Security Services until the fall of 1989. This was discovered after the peaceful revolution. I avoided all contact with congregational members because of shame about my activity as an informer. I did not want to be approached.

I found a place behind a pillar, where I felt secure. The church was completely filled. When the choir entered and took their place in the chancel, I discovered many familiar faces. I felt painfully how lonely I had become during the last years.

The mighty entrance chorus gripped me: "Rejoice, be glad! Rise! Praise the days! Laud what the Most High has done today! Stop fearing, banish the complaining..."

I forgot everything around me. I closed my eyes and listened. All six cantatas were on the program, somewhat shortened. The choir and orchestra and soloists took turns or made music together. I was as if in ecstasy. Eventually I awakened again and became more conscious of the text. I could read it in the program. I became suddenly alert by the sixth cantata.

---

1. Hartmann is referring to the *Christmas Oratorio* of Johann Sebastian Bach (1685–1750).

The Three Informers of King Herod

What task did King Herod give the three Magi from the Orient? "Go and search diligently for the little child, and when you find him, tell me again, so that I can come as well and worship him!"[2]

I was acquainted with such orders. Did King Herod use the Magi as informers? Did he bribe them or even blackmail them? Herod was capable of anything!

However, the story ends well. God shows them another return route in a dream. The three Magi do not have to give any informer reports.

The oratorio now ended very quickly. I again became very anxious. After all, I did not want to be recognized. I was able to exit the church quickly through a side exit.

A pleasant coolness with a bit of rain welcomed me outside. I breathed deeply. Then I began to ponder again. Why did God not send a messenger to me who led me on detours past the State Security Service? I was suddenly addressed at a street crossing. "I was glad to see you in our church once again." It was Dr. N. who addressed me in such a friendly manner, of all people Dr. N. about whom I wrote quite a few reports. He must have noticed my internal perturbance. He invited me to drink a cup of tea with him with such great warmth that I could not decline the invitation. When his wife joined us two hours later—as a member of the choir she had celebrated the successful performance with the choir—everything that was important had been expressed between me and Dr. N. God had sent Dr. N. to me, and he showed me how I should proceed. Thus, like the three Magi from the Orient, I returned home by another way.

2. See Matt 2:8.

1999

An Encounter on Children's Day[1]

I AM SITTING AT a bus stop at the Dessau train station. I bought some little things for the grandchildren for Children's Day. Also for the parents. They also still want to be seen as children, at least on Children's Day.

An older man sits down next to me with difficulty, apparently wholly exhausted. He closes his eyes. I can observe him without being disturbed. He has a nice head, tanned, short white hair, even features that look relaxed. However, this is deceiving. A few moments later the man is greatly agitated. He rummages about in his pants pockets and counts ten-pfennig coins and pennies. Is there enough for a ticket? Should I give him two Marks? But I do not want to shame him.

Women and men, who are waiting for the bus, sit and stand all around him. I notice how worn out and dirty his clothes are. Is he a homeless person who spends the nights somewhere in a niche of a house or in a public park?

He stands up suddenly, staggering a bit, and clears a way through the waiting people. Startled, they retreat and make room for him in the direction of the train station and stare after him full of indignation and disgust. Now I also discover it. The man filled his pants. Everything is wet and smeared.

He has barely disappeared when it becomes loud among those waiting. "Such a filthy mess! In broad daylight! The man should be ashamed of himself! Such people should not be tolerated on public transportation! . . ."

1. The Kindertag or International Children's Day is typically celebrated annually on June 1, although some countries observe the day on another date. A commitment to fostering the welfare and legal rights of children is the particular focus of the day.

An Encounter on Children's Day

No one knew the man. Did he want to use the toilet in the train station with the few ten-pfennig coins that he found in his pockets? Was he sick with a urinary tract or a digestive system illness caused by having to be outside overnight in the cold? Does he even dare go to a doctor with such dirty clothes? Does he have health insurance? Where can he take a shower? Where can he use a washing machine for his clothes? Can he buy a new set of clothes in a clothing store? Questions, questions! However, these questions did not seem to affect those waiting. Some continued to complain about the "pig." Most were silent, as I was, or they had found other subjects of conversation.

This stranger was also a child once. Surely he also has children and grandchildren. However, do they know where he lives and under what circumstances? What profession did he learn once upon a time? How long has he been unemployed? Did his unemployment lead to his social decline?

Our bus arrives. We enter it. Acquaintances chat with one another about vacation, garden, weather, and sickness.

We celebrated the Children's Day in our garden in the afternoon with the small and adult children.

The stranger who was also a child once, where was he? Where did he creep away like a shy animal?

2000

A Fifty-year Reunion

FROM A LETTER TO a fellow student who could not participate:

Most of us probably did not think that this would still be possible, but we met in Aschersleben fifty years after our graduation. Unfortunately, you could not participate. However, we thought about you and want to convey warm greetings from all of us.

Our paths of life have led us far apart. Many of us went to West Germany. The rest of us remained in the East. Each of us went her or his own way with regard to family, professionally, politically, ideologically.

We had successes, had to cope with defeats, and were challenged to pursue new beginnings. We experienced private happiness, but were also not spared human affliction.

And yet we were together again, recognized each other, understood each other, and agreed in the conviction that our school days in Aschersleben were a help in our lives, particularly because so much was happening at that time. Teachers and students searched for new directions. What radical changes we already experienced during our school days. Some of us had already begun our education in the Stephaneum or in the Lyceum[1] in 1942 and remained in the same class with some of our fellow students until our graduation. New students were always added during the war and during the post-war years and also left again. We participated in the destinies of

---

1. The Lyceum was a secondary school for girls and was an equivalent of the Gymnasium. The Stephaneum was a Gymnasium. It dates its history back to 1325 CE and still exists.

A Fifty-year Reunion

teachers and students. Many of us existentially suffered bomb attacks, the misery of being refugees, hunger, and the most serious illnesses.

Hopes and visions for life formation and for new social orders were awakened in us during these school days. There was also much happy light-heartedness and exuberance among us in these difficult years after the war, which is a privilege of children and youth in every age!

We talked about all of these things fifty years after our graduation. There was not enough time. However, we think that many conversations will continue. Perhaps there will be other class reunions.

We thought about the deceased from our graduating class with emotion.

You can recognize who participated in this class reunion from the enclosed photo.

We want to encourage you to stay in contact with us.

I greet you sincerely in the name of Class 12a.

2001

Suddenly Gone

FROM A CHRISTMAS LETTER to our friends:

An Evangelical pastor from the USA whom we had met forty-one years ago in a Baptist church in Moscow writes to us in these days: "We wish for our government that it could ask itself the question: Why does our foreign policy call forth so much hatred in the world? We wish that the terrorists will be captured and that future terrorism will be prevented. However, we also need a lasting change of heart."

A television program about the peace movement in the USA has shown us that our friend is not alone in his opinion. The longing for a realm of peace breaks through ever anew in spite of innumerable setbacks. When we are alarmed today by the activities of the Islamic fundamentalists, who want to erect a theocracy with the use of force, we should, however, not forget how often Christians succumbed to this temptation in the course of history. During the past months we had an impressive exhibition in Magdeburg about Emperor Otto[1] and his time. Those of us from Sachsen-Anhalt were proud that we could show the visitors from all German federal states and also many Europeans and Americans that important chapters of German and European history were already written in our region one thousand years ago, also important chapters of church history. However, was the

---

1. Otto I (912–973) was the Duke of Saxony and became German King from 936 until 973 and Holy Roman Emperor from 962 until 973. He expanded his dynastic power significantly, curbed the power of other German nobles, defeated the Magyars, conquered Italy, gained authority over the church, and fostered an intellectual and artistic renaissance.

Suddenly Gone

Holy Roman Empire of the German nation the realm that was established in view of the birth of the child from Bethlehem? Since the time that Emperor Constantine[2] elevated the Christian religion to be the state religion (in the fourth century), the church has succumbed to the temptation to assume a powerful role in a Christian theocracy. Christ was taken up to heaven as the Pantocrator. The "Christian emperor" ruled on earth with cross and sword, and the bishops of the church were his most loyal fellow combatants. The Christian religion was propagated through crusades. Wars decided whether neighboring tribes were subjected to the German Empire and, thereby, at the same time to the Christian church.

However, there was also opposition in the churches to this Christian theocracy during every century because it contradicted the messages of the New Testament.

Christiane and I heard about the terrible events of September 11 on a bus. We were on a trip from Florence to La Verna, an old monastery in a secluded mountain countryside. Francis of Assisi[3] lived in this monastery with his friends for many years. They wanted to protest against the wealth and power of the church with their order. During a time when there were bloody rivalries in Tuscany—one city against another, the supporters of the emperor against the supporters of the pope—Francis lived here with his friars[4] in the quiet monastery. They remembered Jesus's Sermon on the Mount and sought to practice love of the enemy and reconciliation.

As we entered the monastery, dejected and startled because of the news reports that we heard from the USA, and moved up and down over steep steps on the rocks, in secluded recesses, in the cloister, and in the modest church, we remembered texts that are traced back to a prayer of Francis: "O Lord, make me an instrument of your peace, that I practice love where there is hate; that I forgive where there is insult; that I light a candle where darkness rules..."

---

2. Emperors Constantine I (272–337) and Licinius (263–325) announced the toleration of Christianity in the Edict of Milan in 313 CE. Emperors Theodosius I (347–395), Gratian (359–383), and Valentinian II (371–392) declared Christianity to be the official religion of the Roman Empire with the Edict of Thessalonica in 380 CE.

3. Francis of Assisi (1181/82–1226) is an admired spiritual leader of the Christian community who founded the Order of Friars Minor or the Franciscans. He was particularly interested in serving people with obvious needs but respected the whole natural environment and all of God's creatures. He was also an advocate of apostolic poverty.

4. The original reads Mönche. The translation is "friars" rather than "monks" because the former is a more accurate term for the Franciscans.

The Quest for Faithfulness

It is amazing how such old texts can suddenly become relevant. Shortly after our return from Tuscany we heard the symphony concert "Surrogate Cities" by Heiner Goebbels[5] in the Dessau Theater. The symphony had its premiere ten years ago in Frankfurt on the Main. We were deeply moved as we heard the texts, as if they had been written after the events of September 11, 2001.[6]

However, another city has helped us to cope again. On December 8 we experienced the Advent Motet in the overcrowded St. Thomas Church in Leipzig. The choral motet by Johannes Brahms,[7] "O Savior, tear the heavens open . . ." impressed us particularly:

> Sprout forth, oh earth, sprout forth, oh earth,
> so that mountain and valley all become green!
> Oh earth, bring forth the little flower,
> Oh Savior, spring forth from the earth!

This hopeful text originates from the Roman Catholic theologian Friedrich Spee,[8] who fought passionately and courageously and successfully against the dreadful practice of witch trials.

We pass this on at Christmas from one friend to another, every year anew:

The king of peace from Bethlehem does not allow Himself to be defeated by any power.

---

5. Heiner Goebbels (b. 1952) has been a prolific German composer and performer, including with the rock group Cassiber. He is particularly known as a composer of ensemble works, works for large orchestras, and stage works. He has also been a professor at the University of Giessen and at the European Graduate School in Saas-Fee, Switzerland. His musical productions have been performed throughout the world.

6. The text in this Geobbels work, originally from a novel by Paul Auster, expresses the ephemeral nature of things we have seen and taken for granted, but which can disappear suddenly.

7. Johannes Brahms (1833–1897) was one of the most influential composers of the nineteenth century, and his works for piano, organ, voice, and symphony orchestra continue to be performed and admired. He had exceptional skills as a pianist and also produced many folk songs.

8. Friedrich Spee (1591–1635) was a Jesuit priest, professor, and hymn writer. He transcended the mentality of his time by opposing witchcraft trials and the use of torture to obtain confessions from people. While he did not deny the existence of witches, he was concerned that individuals were falsely accused and suffered as a result. He also insisted that torture does not necessarily result in the discovery of truth. Indeed, people in pain will often admit what is desired and also make accusations against innocent people in order to escape further torture.

2002

A Good Conclusion

"Our life lasts seventy years, and if it is longer, it is eighty years; and if it was delightful, it was trouble and work . . ."[1] This is how Martin Luther translates Psalm 90 from the first millennium BCE.

Seventy years are a very long time for me, and forty-three of those I lived together with my wife. What have the two of us not experienced together, with our children and grandchildren, on our travels, and during the many moves and constantly new beginnings! How many interesting people did we meet! How many revolutionary changes have surprised us! Sometimes we also participated a bit in them. And there were always new situations in which we had to find our way. We do not want to conceal that the years of service in the church were sometimes difficult and required too much of us. On the whole, we were fortunate that we could work and help to create something in church and society.

Seventy years are a long time for us personally. From the perspective of history, seventy years are only a brief blink of an eye.

A picture of an unemployed person was published in a Berlin newspaper in the year that we were born. He was standing on the Potsdamer Platz, with a poster in front of his belly: "I am looking for any kind of work." He had pulled his hat deeply down on his face, as if he were ashamed. At that time he was one of 6,127,000 unemployed people in Germany.

---

1. The translation reflects Hartmann's rendering of Luther's translation of Ps 90:10. The latter part of the verse should read ". . . and if it appeared to be delightful, it was still only futile trouble; . . ."

Seventy years later this picture could have been taken in Dessau, Erfurt, Halle, or Dresden. Then he would have been one of four million unemployed people. At the same time, we know that we should actually add an additional one million to this number. After seventy years we are still treading water. Is there no solution to this problem?

When we demanded in Erfurt after the Wende that the right to work had to be codified in the constitution as a human right, we were ridiculed. No modern country could afford this. The market alone regulates everything by itself. Must it, then, be accepted that thousands or even millions are unemployed periodically or long-term, which means that they live without meaning, and without a goal, and without happiness, and with difficult limitations in daily life?

Must not all of us seventy-year old people pull our caps or hats deep down on our face in shame and admit that we also could not get a grip on what already troubled our parents and grandparents during our seventy or even eighty years? "And if it was delightful, it was trouble and work." The one praying the psalm does not mean this ironically. Work can be burdensome and agonizing. It is more agonizing when people have no work.

We seventy-year-old people want to bequeath this to those who are forty years old today as a legacy. We have preserved for ourselves our vision of a more humane world during all disappointments and all defeats. Therefore we always ventured new beginnings. "A hope learns to walk!" With these words we encouraged each other in the citizen rights groups during the time of the German Democratic Republic. A politician of our time supposedly said: "Whoever comes with visions in the realm of politics can immediately make an appointment with a psychiatrist." I want to confute this person: Whoever dares to enter the field of politics without visions will soon be in danger of losing sight of the most important function of politics, namely, to make society a bit more humane.

At the conclusion of the parabolic piece, *The Good Person of Szechwan*, Bertolt Brecht turns to the audience with the following words. They are also intended to be my words to the generation of our children:

> We know very well that this is no proper conclusion.
> The golden legend had something quite different in mind.
> It secretly accepted a bitter ending.
> Should it be a different human being? Or a different world?
> Perhaps only other gods? Or none?
> We are shattered, and not only for the sake of appearance!

A Good Conclusion

This would be the only way out of this trouble:
They themselves must consider immediately how one can help the good person to achieve a good outcome.
Honored audience, go, find the conclusion yourself!
There must be a good one, must, must, must!

Dear women and men school friends!

Many of us have celebrated our seventieth birthday during these months. I have written "Our Seventy Years—History and Stories"[2] for our children and grandchildren. I have printed out the last chapter for you. I want to greet you with it. Each one of us will have constructed her or his own worldview on the basis of her or his own life experiences. However, perhaps some of us share the hope of Bertolt Brecht, that there must be a good conclusion. The vision of a good human being and a better, more humane society has inspired people in every century to ever-new ventures. Even when the hopes were not fulfilled one hundred percent, there were also always successes and positive changes. However, there was also a disappointing, terrible experience throughout the centuries. When powerful people and nations divided into good ones and bad ones, into just forms of government and rogue states, and sought to liberate the world with force from villains and tyrants, from those who believed differently and dissidents, from those disloyal to a party and traitors, then there were terrible consequences. Not only the revolution devours its children! How many reform movements and attempts at renewal have failed!

Are you acquainted with Brecht's last known verses from the year 1956?

> As I awakened toward morning
> in the white hospital room of the Charité
> and heard the blackbird, I comprehended
> it better. I already had no fear of death for quite some time.
> After all, I can miss nothing, provided
> I myself am missing. Now
> I was able to be glad
> also about all the singing of the blackbird after me.

---

2. This is the title Hartmann gave to his memoir.

The Quest for Faithfulness

I dedicate such hopeful words to all from our graduating class who are already deceased. I wish it for us living that we do not miss hearing the quiet song of the blackbird in the loud din of our time!

Your Helmut Hartmann

Bibliography

Bloch, Ernst. *The Principle of Hope*. Cambridge, MA: MIT Press, 1986.
Bonhoeffer, Dietrich. *The Cost of Discipleship*. Rev. ed. New York: Macmillan, 1963.
———. *Letters and Papers from Prison*. Bethge, Eberhard, editor. Enlarged edition. New York: Macmillan, 1972.
———. *Sanctorum Communio, Dietrich Bonhoeffer Works, Vol 1*. Translated by Reinhard Krauss and Nancy Lukens, edited by Clifford J. Green. Minneapolis: Fortress, 1998.
Brandt, Willy. *Erinnerungen*. 3rd expanded ed. Frankfurt am Main: Propyläen, 1989.
———. *My Life in Politics*. New York: Viking, 1992.
Brecht, Bertolt. "Als ich in weissem Krankenzimmer der Charité," in *Werke. Grosse kommentierte Berliner und Frankfurter Ausgabe*, Band 15: Gedichte 5. Berlin: Suhrkamp, 1989.
———. *Der gute Mensch von Sezuan*, in *Werke. Grosse kommentierte Berliner und Frankfurter Ausgabe*, Band 6: Stücke 6. Berlin: Suhrkamp, 1989.
Fanon, Frantz. *The Wretched of the Earth*. Translated by Constance Farrington. New York: Grove, 1963.
Feuerbach, Ludwig. *The Essence of Christianity*. Mineola, New York: Dover, 2012.
Goes, Albrecht. *The Burnt Offering*. Translated by Michael Hamburger. New York: Pantheon, 1956.
Gollwitzer, Helmut. *Krummes Holz–aufrechter Gang: zur Frage nach dem Sinn des Lebens*. Munich: Chr. Kaiser Ferlag, 1970.
Hamel, Johannes. *Christ in der DDR*. Berlin: Käthe Vogt, 1957.
———. *A Christian in East Germany*. Translated by Ruth and Charles C. West, 2nd ed. London: SCM, 1961.
Hartmann, Heinrich. *Zschokkes Stunden der Andacht*. Gütersloh: Bertelsmann, 1932.
Hromádka, Josef Lukl. *Sprung über die Mauer: ein Hromádka Lesebuch*. Wuppertal: P. Hammer, 1991.
Klepper, Jochen. *Der Vater: Roman des Soldatenkönigs*. E-artnow, 2018 [1935].
Kühn, Alfred. *Die Materie in Atomen und Sternen*. Berlin: Wegweiser, 1934.
Lenz, Siegfried. *The German Lesson*. Translated by Ernst Kaiser and Eithne Wilkins. New York: New Direction, 1986. (Original: *Deutschstunde*. Hamburg: Ganske, 1968.)
———. *So zärtlich war Sulejken*. Hamburg: Hoffman und Campe, 1955.
Lessing, Gotthold Ephraim. *Nathan the Wise, with Related Documents*. Translated, edited, and with an introduction by Ronald Schechter. Boston: Bedford/St. Martin's, 2004. Other earlier editions are available.

Bibliography

Luther, Martin, *Luthers Werke, Kritische Gesamtausgabe, Schriften.* Knaake, J. F. K., et al., eds. 73 vols. Weimar: Böhlau, 1883–2009. Referred to as WA in footnotes.

Luther, Martin. *Luther's Works.* Lehmann, Helmut, and Pelikan, Jaroslav, eds. 55 vols. Philadelphia: Fortress; St. Louis: Concordia, 1955–1986. Referred to as LW in footnotes.

Repgow, Eike of. "*Der Verfasser.*" In *Der Sachsenspiegel/Eike von Repgow.* Schott, Clausdieter, editor. Translation of Landrecht by Ruth Schmidt-Wiegand; epilogue and translation of Lehenrecht by Clausdieter Schott. 3rd rev. ed. Manesse-Bibliothek der Weltliteratur (in German). Zürich: Manesse (Random House), 2006 [1475].

Weckerling, Rudolf. *Durchkreutzer Hass. Vom Abenteuer des Friedens.* (*Crossed-out Hatred: Concerning the Adventure of Peace.*) Berlin: Vogt, 1961.

www.ingramcontent.com/pod-product-compliance
Lightning Source LLC
Chambersburg PA
CBHW071444150426
43191CB00008B/1235